WILL THE REAL YOU PLEASE STAND UP

WILL THE REAL YOU PLEASE STAND UP

SHOW UP, BE AUTHENTIC, AND PROSPER IN SOCIAL MEDIA

KIM GARST

NEW YORK

WILL THE REAL YOU PLEASE STAND UP

Show Up, Be Authentic, and Prosper in Social Media

Published in New York, New York, by Morgan James Publishing. Morgan James and The Entrepreneurial Publisher are trademarks of Morgan James, LLC.
www.MorganJamesPublishing.com

ISBN 978-1-63047-270-2 paperback
ISBN 978-1-63047-271-9 eBook
ISBN 978-1-63047-272-6 hardcover
Library of Congress Control Number: 2014940590

Cover Design by:
Rachel Lopez
www.r2cdesign.com

Interior Design by:
Bonnie Bushman
bonnie@caboodlegraphics.com

CONTENTS

INTRODUCTION
AUTHENTICITY—THE NEW STANDARD IN MARKETING

In late 1994, Quaker Oats was fresh off the success of building Gatorade from a small, special-purpose athletic drink into a multibillion-dollar beverage brand. Quaker Oats Chairman William D. Smithburg then turned his attention to another beverage brand, hoping to repeat his success. That year Quaker Oats acquired the iconic Snapple for $1.7 billion, gaining a company built on low-budget, charming advertising. If the $1.7 billion brand could be built around "The Snapple Lady," imagine what the marketing wizards at Quaker Oats could do once they got their hands on the company.

Four years after the acquisition, Quaker sold Snapple for $300 million, booking a $1.4 billion loss.

What happened?

Many experts blamed the failure on several things: logistical issues, bad bottling contracts, an undeveloped distribution network, and, mostly, overconfident leadership. Do you want my opinion? Quaker failed because it tried to apply a number of "big brand," slick marketing techniques to a company that had been built on an image of being the off-beat, quirky brand of the new generation. People liked that it was a unique alternative to the long-established brands.

This glaring inauthenticity was apparent to Snapple's customers, whose loyalty began to wane. It seemed Snapple's so-called amateur marketing was part of its appeal. Once it was gone, so was the devotion of the people who were committed to it for this very reason.

Compare this to the well-known and beloved story of Steve Jobs returning to Apple in 1997. At the time, Apple products were seen as marginalized, anachronistic, and not mainstream enough. According to Jobs, at his return, Apple was ninety days from bankruptcy. Today, Apple has a higher market valuation than Microsoft. Apple's products have defined a generation of new technology users. In a stunning show of brand loyalty, converts are willing to spend hours in line to be among the first to purchase new product versions, even when there aren't substantial changes in the version.

What's the difference between these two brands? What determines the failure of one iconic brand and the comeback of another?

Authenticity!

I will make the case that authenticity is the game changer, the difference maker, and the "secret sauce" that makes marginal companies good and good companies great. I will help you find your authenticity and learn to weave it into everything your company does. I will show you how to use it not only to find but to cement relationships and turn customers into repeat buying apostles.

Why This Book?

Those who have heard my story know I have been in the social media business since, well, before it was called social media. I have seen the rise of AOL and the fall of Myspace, B2B boards, chat rooms, forums, conversations happening in 140 characters or less, and the juggernaut that is Facebook. Whether they succeeded or failed, all each was trying to do was connect people. However, just connecting people is not enough anymore. We are finding out that having thousands of Facebook "fans" does not mean your company will flourish. Why? Because all connections are not equal. What businesses ***really*** need is to build connections that last, connections that transcend a single product or marketing campaign, connections that span an extended period.

Think about your relationships that have endured year after year. It is not what makes them special in the beginning that creates loyalty; rather, it is what keeps them special over time that matters. What are those things? They are communication, reliability, honesty, and the feeling that both sides are there for each other and can count on each other to be who or what they really are. The problem is many brands do not get this. I see campaign after campaign focused solely on likes, views, fan acquisition, and other quick-hit statistics. Successful social media marketing is not built on "impressions." **It is built on relationships.**

I am not saying I have all the answers, but I can tell you this: My entire online career, all twenty-plus years, has been built around the authentic me. Good, bad, right, or wrong, what you see is what you get, and it has served me well, as I have built successful business after successful business.

If your intent is to build a strong brand, your authenticity and integrity are critical to your success. Don't think you can get away with trying to be something you are not. People can sniff out a fake in a heartbeat today. Bottom line: Somehow, someway, the real you will always shine through.

Brands perceived as authentic have always done well in the marketplace. Consider the case of Ben & Jerry's ice cream, a company that prided itself on making the best ice cream from quality ingredients obtained in a sustainable and ecologically responsible manner. Their story resonates with their customers.

These days the need for brands to be authentic is more important than ever because of the rise of social media.

It's not that social media has changed the definition of *authenticity*; it is just that there are now more and easier opportunities for not just the company, but its customers to influence a brand's image.

So why did I write this book? There are lots of reasons, but there is one underlying reason that really pushed me: **I think there is a better way to use social media and market online!**

Social media has changed the marketing landscape forever. It is no longer a one-way conversation or a bombardment of impression-driven push marketing. It is two-way relationship marketing done at a hyper-accelerated pace with new tools that we never could have imagined twenty years ago. My goal is to help people, companies, and brands learn, use, and ultimately master these tools and concepts to envision, build, scale, and, ultimately, manage large, inter-connected online communities of not just prospects and customers, but brand apostles.

Are you ready for the shocking part? To be successful, you will need to make only ONE significant change, and you can make that change instantly. Sounds easy, right? It is not. It is the one thing I see businesses of all sizes struggle with. To be wildly successful, you are going to need to check your ego, forget any preconceived notions of how you think social media marketing should be done, and—here is the hard part—commit to being yourself online. **To really succeed, I need the real you to stand up in social media.**

CHAPTER 1

WHY AUTHENTICITY?

What is authenticity, and what does it mean to be authentic? There are a number of definitions of "authenticity," depending on whether you look at the dictionary or some of the many bloggers online who have contributed to an evolving understanding of authenticity in the marketplace. Dictionary.com defines "authenticity" as "undisputed credibility." If credibility means being trusted, then undisputed credibility is a deep abiding level of trust that is not to be taken lightly. Abuses are devastating for those who have placed their trust in the person or brand entity trusted.

Popular writer and marketer Seth Godin calls authenticity "doing what you promise," rather than the vague idea of "being who you are." He clarifies that he talks about *doing* rather than *being* because *doing* is something clearly obvious to all. *Being*, on the other hand, is sometimes difficult to evaluate because it requires long-term observation and complex processing. In other words, I do not know if you are punctual by nature, but if we had ten opportunities to meet at a specific time and place and you were there on time all ten, I would conclude that you are not only punctual, but reliable, at least from a time commitment standpoint. There is an old saying, "Actions speak louder than words," and this is a true testament to being authentic.

The obviousness of doing is a useful measure for authenticity. It becomes clear to your audience if the things you are doing match up with the things you say you believe and the things you say you will do. A mismatch between the things you do and the things you say is

"Figure out who you are; then do it on purpose."

evidence of being inauthentic, and being inauthentic is something most people do not tolerate online anymore. Here is a major difference now, though: In the past, the offended person would fade away and not do business with you anymore. Now the person uses social media to tell everybody he or she can about how you treated, or didn't treat, them. In a matter of hours, viral dings to your brand image become a real possibility.

Country singer Dolly Parton said something I love: "Figure out who you are; then **do it on purpose**."

What does it mean to "figure out who you are"? It means taking the time to identify your strengths, weaknesses, talents, values, and interests, and all the things that make you uniquely you. Notice I am saying the word "you" a lot. Figuring out who you are and being true to yourself is not just important, but it is critical to being authentic. Consistency is a fundamental part of being authentic, and the only way to assure consistency is to take the possibility of fabrication out of your decision-making. It is not hard to figure out what to post, share, comment on, or like when you do not have to think about it because you are being who you are. Most people work exactly the opposite way. They try to figure out who and what other people want them to be, and then create a false persona to support their preconceived notion of what that imaginary personality would do. This approach has to be exhausting!

Now let's move this concept into the business world. I have seen marketing study after marketing study done to create a company's new brand image. "Do this, that, and the other thing to be cooler, hip, and appealing to the eighteen to thirty-four demographic." From there, products are built, advertising campaigns are launched, social media platforms are constructed, and a new, imaginary version of the company is created. It is ultimately a lie. It never works, and people see right through it. Sorry, Buick; in spite of the fact that you have spent millions of dollars to have Tiger Woods and Shaquille O'Neal pitch your products, we are always going to think of you as our parents' and grandparents' car company.

Gaining clarity with respect to your strengths, weaknesses, and talents enables you to be authentic in every aspect of your business and branding. It enables you to be authentic in the content you produce, whether on social media, your company website, your marketing materials, or something else. It even enables you to be authentic in the way you dress when meeting with clients.

How do you know when you are building a business and a brand that expresses authenticity to your customers? Among other things, if you are able to summarize what you and your brand stand for in just a few words, likely you have a strong degree of authenticity in your branding and business. On the other hand, if you have a vague concept of what your brand means and what you stand for, and you are not able to articulate it in a few words or sentences, likely you have additional work to do to understand your strengths and talents and how to best package them into an authentic brand message.

When you know what the key message of your brand is and what your brand promises to its customers and prospects, it is easy for you to bring this message to the world with a great deal of confidence, no matter what media you are using—social media, print media, or other methods of marketing. Frankly, it also takes a lot less energy to be authentic than to be inauthentic. When you are authentic, when what you are *doing* matches what you *promise*, it doesn't feel false, and you don't spend your energy worrying about how to ***appear*** more genuine to your audience. You just ***are*** genuine to your audience.

What Authenticity Isn't

Some people, in the name of "authenticity," decide it's okay to engage in behavior that's crass, rude, and utterly offensive. After all, they are just "keeping it real."

Unless the entirety of your brand image centers on a persona that is, in fact, crass, rude, and utterly offensive, then you are not being authentic. It is just plain bad manners. Being authentic does not mean you can say whatever you like, whenever you like, and disregard the consequences of your words and actions.

Everything you say, everything you do, everything you post, every group you join, every photo or meme you share, and everyone you associate with publicly impacts the image your brand represents online. If there is any doubt in your mind whether you would want a prospective client to read what you are writing, the rule is simple: Don't write it. If you wouldn't want your minister, grandma, or children to read it after it has gone public, it's not appropriate to post, and it's likely not an authentic representation of yourself or your brand.

On the other hand, maybe that ***is*** who you are. Consider the example of the blog posts by J. C. Kendall of TekPersona. TekPersona's mission is to help you convert your audience into customers. Kendall's blog is titled *Curmudgeon Musings from Technologist and Marketing Geek*, and to say it's curmudgeonly is putting it nicely. His blog is blunt, brutal, and to the point. The difference is this: It's not the kind of blog that offends for the sake of offending. It's simply his attempt to provide a true sense of who he is, in both his professional and personal life.

> "I like to say that nobody buys anything important from a stranger except for gasoline and Gummi Bears. If you cannot give your audience a sense of who you truly are and gain acceptance for same, good luck getting them to sign on the dotted line."
>
> J.C. Kendall

In an interview with Inc.com, Kendall states, "I like to say that nobody buys anything important from a stranger except for gasoline and Gummi Bears. If you cannot give your audience a sense of who you truly are and gain acceptance for same, good luck getting them to sign on the dotted line."

I might sound like I have contradicted myself, but here is what I am getting at: If you have promised this kind of unabashed honesty, no holds barred, to your audience, then by all means it is exactly what you should deliver.

But if you haven't promised your customers a ride that exciting from the get-go, it is unfair and inauthentic to suddenly change the tone of your content and expect them to hang on for the ride.

Of course, there will be days when you are off. There will be days when something's got your attention and you feel cranky. There will be days when something frustrates you and you want to vent your frustration to the world via a rant. That's normal and natural, and finding a respectful way to express your feelings without openly criticizing someone or another business can be a healthy, authentic choice, to a point. But if criticizing and complaining does not match up to the brand identity you have presented to your audience throughout your marketing materials online and offline, then it is inauthentic (at best) to go off on a tirade, to bash another person or company, or to be excessively negative on a regular basis.

Remember, everything you say, post, and do is a reflection of your brand identity. Because of this, you are, in fact, in the fishbowl, on display all the time. A commitment to authenticity demands a seamless integration among all aspects of the message you present in the name of your brand.

I love that at the end of the day, I don't have to worry about whether what I am saying sounds like me or not. I don't have to waste my energy wondering if my message matches with the image I am projecting. I know I am being me, and I know the things I am doing match up with what I have promised my audience I will do.

Who Judges Authenticity?

This is going to get boring and dry for just a few paragraphs, but hang with me because I think it is important to understand how social media has dramatically changed the traditional marketing landscape.

Historically in the world of marketing, brand image has been understood as a characteristic that resides in the perception of the customer. In marketing courses, this has been called either the customer-based brand equity (CBBE) model or mind-share model. In the CBBE model, knowledge of a brand is the key to building brand equity. Brand knowledge is built through reinforcing brand image and brand awareness with customers.

Within this model, building a strong brand involves multiple sequential steps in a ladder kind of arrangement. It involves shaping how customers think, feel, and act with respect to a particular brand. An assortment of "brand building blocks" are put together in a logical fashion, identifying strengths and weaknesses, and providing shape

> You need to first realize that people have an instant, 360-degree view of your company, and make sure your message is crafted and delivered consistently and authentically everywhere you exist online.

for further marketing activities. These building blocks progress from a simple understanding of your brand identity—for example, answering the question "Who am I as a brand?"—all the way to answering questions like, "What is my relationship with this brand?" The desired customer actions within this model range from brand awareness to a deep loyalty to a particular brand.[1]

Screech!

All of that has changed now. Thanks to social media, relationships are not spoon-fed by brands in nice little increments anymore, and the flow is no longer unidirectional. People now have the ability to go from never having heard of a particular brand to getting enough information about that brand to form a lasting impression of it in a matter of minutes. Forget websites and emails and nice little cleverly scripted marketing messages. People can use Facebook, Twitter, and a number of other sites to see what the "real deal" is on companies from people they

1 http://www.mindtools.com/pages/article/keller-brand-equity-model.htm

know and trust and the community as a whole, not the company itself.

Brands are now more transparent than they ever have been, and not because they want to be. It's the nature of social media. So if you want to create a positive brand image, you need to first realize that people have an instant 360-degree view of your company, and make sure your message is crafted and delivered consistently and authentically everywhere you exist online.

Why Does Your Audience Want You to Be Authentic?

Customers are longing for businesses to make a claim and be what they say they are—no more, no less. With the unprecedented transparency social media provides, businesses cannot hide behind their marketing departments for marketing message control. Your company and brand message has to be filled with sincerity, trust, and unity with the actions of your company, or you are likely to have one of those social media mishaps in which an unfortunate display of inauthentic behavior by a company suddenly goes viral. It is word-of-mouth marketing on steroids. This kind of safe connection around a brand and its message can make or break a brand's reputation.

Let's think for a second about brands that have made a claim to who they are and behave consistently in line with that image generation after generation: *Star Trek*, Apple, Harley-Davidson, Starbucks, and Coca-Cola. Years after the end of the television series and its multiple spinoffs, *Star Trek* conventions continue to gather thousands of devoted fans. The Apple experience draws people from all walks of life who are willing to spend hours in line for every new product release, even without significant technological advances, solely to be part of the Apple experience. Harley-Davidson events, such as the annual Sturgis rally, draw together wealthy urban businessmen, working-class lifestyle bikers, and even people who don't normally ride motorcycles, to name a few, on a recurring basis in celebration of this legendary brand. Starbucks created comfy lounges, where its customers can mingle and meet one another and begin making the story of this brand their own.

In short, people want their favorite brands to be authentic so they know what to expect from them, what they can count on.

Chapter 2

HOW DO YOU CREATE AUTHENTICITY? TELLING YOUR BRAND'S STORY

In *Fortune* magazine's October 22, 2007, issue, Angela Ahrendts, then CEO of Burberry, articulated a key element of her brand's success. She remarked: "Our goal is not to be Hermès or Bottega Veneta. Britishness is so much a part of what we're about—now let's do that better than anyone else in the world."

Clearly, Ms. Ahrendts understands a fundamental characteristic of an authentic brand—it knows and clings to its defining traits.

By knowing and clinging to the roots of your brand, you connect your brand to its past as well as to the larger cultural context in which your brand is situated. This sounds like such an easy, almost trivial thing to accomplish, but it is not. It is not that Ms. Ahrendts understood what the true cornerstone of her business was that drove the brand's success. It was that she was "all in" on making sure that message was woven into everything the company did.

The process of crafting and sharing the story of a brand is the perfect medium through which a brand articulates and clings to its roots. It is the lens through which all other marketing innovations must be examined for faithfulness to the heritage of the brand. Notice I didn't say history. Clinging only to the history of a brand could result in a stubborn refusal to innovate or adapt, and could prove limiting for a brand.

The heritage of a brand, however, is a different story. A brand's heritage is the feelings associated with the historical context of a brand's story. Being authentic as a marketer means you ensure the content of your brand's story is consistent with the feelings you are trying to evoke in telling the story of your brand.

Making a commitment to ***be*** authentic is entirely different from making a commitment to simply ***appear*** more authentic. By this I mean it is not enough for a marketing team or CEO to consider the question, "How do we appear more authentic to our customers?" Authenticity must be a value communicated to, communicated by, and demonstrated by every member of an organization, whether a Fortune 500 company or a small, newly formed one-person operation.

This should make it apparent that traditional marketing models and activities are not designed to build the authenticity and transparency that customers have come to expect from their brand. In addition, traditional marketing activities could, in fact, damage the authenticity of the company if the message presented does not align with the everyday activities of the company.

In looking at the ways brands communicate their values and authenticity in an era of Internet-driven marketing, a number of practices appear to be common among brands consumers perceive as having a great deal of authenticity. First and foremost among these practices is understanding the power of storytelling. It might be cliché, but it is still true: Words tell; stories sell.

It is rare that someone makes a buying decision based on the features and benefits of a product. It is not about the price point, it is not about the advertising channels, and it is really not about the facts. It is about the stories the brand tells and the emotional connection that people make with the product or service being marketed. The only way the story the brand tells will be believed, at least in the long run (and your brand's product or service sold), is if it is true.

In all honesty, marketers tell stories because this is how people expect to get their information about a product. A bulleted list of features and benefits would not have the power of narrative that suggests to a customer how this product will make him or her feel or look better. People buy because they want the emotion associated with the product. The best indicator of how you might feel about something you buy is through the stories the company tells you and, even better, through the stories others who have tried the product or service tell.

Understanding which pieces of a brand story to tell to which audience, in what order, and in which place is a large part of the marketing puzzle. In the age of social media, this is properly understood not just as the domain of the marketing team. Authentic (and socially savvy) organizations understand that this is the work of everyone involved in an organization. It is work that is essential to communicating a brand's authenticity to its customers.

To communicate a brand's story in a way that gains the most benefit, it is important to understand a few things about your customers and their perceptions before you begin storytelling throughout your brand message.

Know Your Customers' Perspectives

An authentic story considers the customers perspectives before it even begins. By this I mean a brand story is not an attempt to change a customer's perception or perspective. A brand story that is authentic stands on its own and is respectful of the reality that the customer's story also stands on its own. Trying to compete with a customer's preexisting perspective sets an environment of mistrust and hostility and is never a good method of telling an authentic brand story.

One of the ways of telling a brand story that considers the customers' perspectives is to identify and understand the values that are important to the customers and, as long as these values are shared in a way that will be seamless and authentic, frame the story by giving reference to these values.

For example, the outdoor gear supplier Patagonia includes environmental awareness and activism as important corporate values within its customer base. These values are shared by a great majority of Patagonia's customers. As a company, Patagonia chooses not to market with companies that don't share the same values. More specifically, Patagonia chooses not to market using traditional media, such as print, television, and radio ads, to support this brand philosophy.

The story the Patagonia brand tells of being a highly principled company that chooses not to profit from media it deems objectionable and contrary to its stated values tells the story of a brand that chooses ethics over traditional understandings of the easiest way to profit. This story resonates with Patagonia's customers, and, in fact, word-of-mouth advertising and customer loyalty are the core drivers of Patagonia's growth.

First Impressions Matter

A brand story must be authentic from the first moment a customer encounters it. First impressions matter and can enhance your brand's ability to communicate authenticity. On the other hand, inattention to the first impression of your brand can damage its authenticity and force you to spend precious marketing time and money combating a poor first impression.

Authenticity is created when marketers of a brand create and communicate a story that customers believe. Once the customers believe the story, they enter it and, in fact, tell it to themselves. One of the marks of a high level of authenticity of a brand occurs when the brand's story becomes so powerful and real to its customers that they share that story with others.

There is a reason that over the past few years major brands have increasingly embraced the power of

storytelling. With such job titles as chief evangelist at major corporations, it is clear that demonstrating authenticity through the telling of a brand's story is becoming obvious to more and more companies.

One of the easiest ways to destroy the authenticity of a brand is to become confused about who owns a brand and its message. In traditional marketing models, marketers owned the message of a brand. The expense of advertising created a high barrier to entry when it came to communicating using mass media. Mass media was a unidirectional model of communication. The brand spoke, and people listened.

CEOs and marketers who believe they are in control of the message of a brand in today's social world will kill the authenticity of that brand. Brands no longer own their message. They can try to control it, but they do not own it. Today, consumers own the message. What they say about a brand carries more weight than what the brand says about itself.

***"Brands no longer own their message.
They can try to control it, but they do not own it.
Today, consumers own the message.
What they say about a brand carries more weight than what the brand says about itself."***

Qualities of Authentic Brands and Their Stories

Sometimes people who are asked to think of just what it is that makes up a brand will identify the exterior symbols of the brand as its core features. It is true that brands use such items as logos, slogans, and images (among others) to communicate the meaning of a brand and its story to consumers. But that is just the tip of the iceberg. A company's slogan, logo, colors, or other image is not, in itself, its brand.

Some of the things that make up a brand include the value it provides its consumers, the potential it communicates to customers, the usefulness of its products or services to fix some pain customers experience, the most desirable benefits and the feelings associated with them that consumers experience, and so on. More than the symbols of the brand, the brand is made up of all the feelings and emotions associated with that brand that customers have.

Leadership

The perception of authenticity at the senior levels of a company is a critical component of the brand's overall authenticity in the marketplace. Think of Steve Jobs of Apple, Bill Gates of Microsoft, or Vince Lombardi of the Green Bay Packers. We might not like or agree with their business management, motivational skills, or politics, but we feel we know (or knew) who they are (or were) as people. Every time we saw or heard about them in public, we pretty much got what we expected from them. In other words, we got their authentic selves.

Brands with strong leaders enjoy increased views of their authenticity, while brands with weaker leaders appear to be less authentic to customers. When considering the leadership of the company as a factor impacting its authenticity, there is an expectation of a high level of passion and commitment to the brand that is exemplified by a consistent result of product or brand excellence.

Originality

Originality refers to the novelty and uniqueness of the concept behind the brand, either its product or service or the way that product or service is delivered to the market. For new entrepreneurs, striving for originality can be a somewhat challenging and elusive concept. How do you think of something that hasn't been thought of before? If coming up with new ideas, new products to solve a problem, or new means of marketing isn't in your experience, it can be intimidating to try to come up with something that satisfies the requirement for novelty and originality as a factor determining authenticity.

The difficulty in coming up with a method for achieving originality isn't just a result of an entrepreneur being new to the art of innovation. It is actually inherent in the concept of originality itself. By its very nature, there can be no one-size-fits-all formula for originality or authenticity. Originality is a product of venturing into new territory, something each brand must navigate for itself.

Then again, some people might argue that there is no such thing as authenticity or originality anymore. Every idea is somehow shaped and created by ideas that preceded it.

No matter your philosophical take on the idea of originality, consumers still believe in it as an ideal, and their understanding of your brand's degree of originality affects their judgment of your brand as either authentic or inauthentic. Originality in marketing can be sparked by looking at an existing product or its delivery in a new way. One method of doing this might be to consider your strengths and talents, and see if there is a way they might obviously be used to create a product or tweak an existing product or service that hasn't been done yet in the marketplace, or certainly not to saturation.

Personally, I think brands can craft their own unique messages regardless of what has come before them if they stay true to their core values and remember whom they serve.

Sincerity

As I mentioned earlier, customers' beliefs about the authenticity of a brand also can be affected by the sincerity with which a brand practices the values it preaches, even in the face of adversity. In the case of Patagonia, its commitment to environmental stewardship has caused it to seek nontraditional advertising venues to practice its values consistently.

Another example, the fast-food chain Chick-fil-A closes its doors on Sundays as a means of sincerely practicing the values expressed by the company's founder. While some people might only focus on the lost profit, Chick-fil-A believes it will be a stronger company if its franchisees and their employees are ensured a regular day of rest and refreshment.

The sincerity of a brand is measured in the consistency of its message to customers as well as to its own people. The brand values, core beliefs, plans, and meaning are all the same, regardless of the audience.

Brands whose sincerity contributes to their authenticity live up to the story they tell about themselves and the stories their customers are eager to spread about them.

Unfortunately, it's often the case that a brand's sincerity—and its customers—are sacrificed in the pursuit of "great marketing." After all, it is easier for companies to create hype than it is to invest time and money into developing a great product with great service to accompany it.

A brand's sincerity is a key issue in differentiating between two or more companies. It's what separates authentic brands from their inauthentic counterparts in the marketplace. After decades of being overly marketed to with no way of escaping the onslaught, short of becoming a hermit in a cave or exercising Amish-like shunning of technology, today's customers are amazingly savvy about the claims made by brands.

Consumers are tired of being overpromised and under-delivered, and in a marketplace rich with alternatives, they are increasingly able to find companies whose authenticity is refreshing and real.

The sincerity of a brand requires a deep level of buy-in from all levels of the company. This is not achievable as a marketing strategy only. It must be a core operating strategy of a company to work. Sincerity starts by creating a service or a product that provides a solution to a problem or solves a true need in the marketplace. It continues through the quality practices observed in the process of manufacturing the product and is reinforced through the brand stories the official custodians of the brand story tell. The final link in the sincerity chain is the post-sale customer service experience, which must reflect a commitment to true, outstanding service consistent with the company's mission and ideals.

It is critical that a company interested in developing a brand with a high level of sincerity believe wholeheartedly in the claims made about its products. It must be dedicated to providing an extremely high level of customer service that is ultimately focused on the goal of customer satisfaction. "That's not my job" can never be an acceptable answer in a company that practices a high degree of sincerity as part of an overall story of authenticity.

One of the key hallmarks of sincerity in a company is a commitment to integrity in all actions associated with the brand's story, marketing, and promotion, as well as every other decision made in the operations and support services performed in the name of the brand.

If a commitment to sincerity is part of a company's approach to being authentic (and it ought to be), the company will exercise the utmost in transparency if and when something unforeseen happens that might affect its ability to deliver on promises. For a company with a high degree of sincerity, determination and creativity are key factors that allow the brand's authenticity to shine. Despite such challenges, a company dedicated to sincerity will find a way to honor its promises. For any company that cultivates sincerity, the value of its word means everything.

Now, I don't mean this to say that marketing materials created by a company dedicated to sincerity in its brand communications must be boring or passionless. Far from it! The kind of hype I am talking about being contrary to sincerity is the kind of overblown hype that is exaggeration after exaggeration. It's hyperbole, to quote one of my old English teachers. You will know it when you see it—it almost seems like a parody of advertising because it is so overboard in claims that cannot possibly all be true.

Powerful, compelling, and sincere marketing content must be created in a way that it naturally engages the customer, making the content simply irresistible to consider further. I will talk about this more later, but it requires the use of skilled writing, particularly in your headlines and email subject lines, that can pique your customers' curiosity without making you resort to sensational tactics that destroy your credibility.

What are the rewards for companies that practice this kind of radical sincerity as part of their commitment to authenticity? Simply, this kind of sincerity is rewarded in the form of loyalty, free word-of-mouth marketing, and brand evangelism from customers.

Customers who have had the pleasant experience of receiving sincerity from a brand are more likely to be repeat customers as a result. Given the cost of developing new leads versus that of retaining existing customers, this can be huge for a brand's profitability.

This loyalty naturally leads to customers who want to share their positive experience with your brand with everyone they know. Especially in the age of social networking, these positive experiences can take the form of a tweet to thousands of followers, a positive comment left along with their check-in at your business, or a note posted on your wall that tags your business fan page. Regardless of how it is shared, the truth is this: Cultivation of sincerity as part of a culture of authenticity brings the benefit of word-of-mouth marketing for your brand via natural evangelism. People want to share the good news!

Heritage and History

Connecting a brand to its historical roots is another way of increasing a brand's perceived authenticity with its customers. This tells a story of commitment to tradition and of loyalty, hints at the idea of the good old days, and connects the company throughout time and place. In recent years, carmakers have used this method surprisingly well by adopting design cues for current models based on successful models from years past. The reintroduction of iconic models is a further means of connecting an automobile brand with its history. Chrysler's reintroduction of the Hemi engine, not to mention the Charger and Challenger models, is a perfect example of this means of increasing consumers' sense of a brand's authenticity.

On the other hand, a failure to understand and connect with a brand's roots can spell the demise of that brand.

In 1999, Oreo drove its No. 1 competitor, Hydrox, out of the cream-filled sandwich cookie market. This doesn't come as much of a surprise. Oreo is the original, and Hydrox, the knockoff. Oreo had history on its side, while Hydrox came on the scene later. Oreo cookies were produced by a large company; Hydrox was simply a smaller competitor that was unable to keep up with the big guys, except for one small point—none of this is the true story.

Hydrox was actually the original cream-filled sandwich cookie, created in 1908. Oreo didn't make its appearance in the cookie aisle until four years later, in 1912. Nabisco, of course, makes Oreo cookies, while Hydrox was owned by Sunshine Biscuits, which was later bought by Keebler and is now owned by Kellogg's, none of which are exactly considered small corporations.

In blind taste tests, Hydrox was the clear winner over Oreo. Truthfully, the Hydrox sandwich cookie was a better product, holding together much better when dunked in milk (which we all know is the only appropriate test to apply to a sandwich cookie).

So why was Hydrox relegated to permanent "knockoff" status in the minds of consumers?

It was the simple result of failing to leverage that brand history and tell the authentic story of the brand. It didn't share what made it unique in the marketplace, much less what made it better than its competitor in every kind of comparison between the two brands.

Connecting your brand with its history and heritage has a powerful effect on your customers, a fact that is well known by Coca-Cola. In the early to mid-1980s, Coke discovered it was losing market share to Pepsi and decided to introduce a reformulation of its cola in an attempt to regain lost ground.

The launch of New Coke in 1985 continues to be regarded as the single biggest marketing failure (and subsequent success) in history, nearly thirty years later. People hated New Coke and didn't hesitate to let the company know what they thought about the product. Coca-Cola acquiesced to the will of the public and eventually brought back Classic Coke. This was an immensely successful move. It seemed Coke had never been so popular!

One element of the brand's history and heritage that is retained to this day is the shape of the iconic Coke bottle, a symbol of the brand's (and the country's) rich past. Coke continues to produce its products in both glass and plastic versions of this bottle, positioning itself as the truly authentic American brand of cola.

It is important to make the distinction between heritage and history. Without understanding how these two elements of authentic branding differ, it is possible to confuse them and the roles they play.

A brand's history is the factual story of what happened in the life cycle of a particular brand. A brand is created, and hopefully it enjoys a nice long life span filled with many historical developments.

The heritage of a brand, on the other hand, is more complex. The heritage of a brand represents the emotional response a customer has as a result of an interaction with a brand. Heritage, then, is not static and can be shaped as part of crafting a brand's story. That said, attempts to shape the heritage of a brand must be approached with caution and respect for the history of a brand. Otherwise, tinkering with a brand's heritage can backfire, creating mistrust of a brand and damaging its efforts at being authentic with its customers.

Usefulness

Another key element of creating authenticity in marketing your brand is to ensure your brand delivers a high degree of usefulness to your customers. In fact, you want this level of usefulness to be so high that your customers believe they can't live without your brand and the value it provides to their lives.

How can a brand provide value to its customers through its marketing message? I will tell you this much: It is not through blasting a top-down marketing message that is just some variation of "Buy me! Buy me!" and "This is who we are and why we are so great." It's not that there is anything wrong with honestly demonstrating to your customers how you provide value, but after you have clearly demonstrated that value, your customers should be the ones articulating just how great you are!

The usefulness of your brand and its message for consumers can be demonstrated by several types of content marketing. Providing usefulness and value for your customers can be done by giving them how-to tips for something challenging within your niche, encouraging and uplifting them, offering humor, keeping them informed of the latest developments in your field, rounding up a weekly digest of stories that are relevant to your business and customers, and more.

Often in the beginning of creating a new brand, novice entrepreneurs will wonder how on earth they will ever earn a profit if they are constantly giving away tricks of the trade in their field.

When you give away valuable content in your field, one of two things will happen. The people who were going to do the task themselves do so and are grateful to you for having provided the information they needed. Chances are good that when they need something again, they will come to your business, ready to buy because of the trust you fostered in giving them great content that was highly valuable and that boosted your authenticity to them.

On the other hand, you might give valuable information to someone who thinks he or she wants to do the thing you have just taught him or her to do, but once the person gets into it, he or she realizes just how complicated it is and that his or her time is much better spent in some other aspect of their business.

Who are these types of people going to call when it is time to outsource? You! By providing them with top-quality, expert advice in your field, you have set yourself apart from your competitors as the go-to person in your niche who has an abundance of experience and information related to the job at hand.

You can't ask for a better marketing outcome than that!

It seems counterintuitive, but you really can't overdo it when it comes to giving top-quality information to your customers. Any way you look at it, you come out of it looking like the professional you are, so confident in your knowledge and business that you can take the time to provide specific, valuable information for your customers and prospects.

What are some of the keys to developing useful content for consumers? It helps to begin with a clear understanding of who your customers and prospects are. It is hard to provide information that is useful without knowing the answer to the question "Useful to whom?"

Start with your customer in mind. Take the time to discover what your customers are looking for, and provide that kind of content to them. Getting to know your customer in the kind of detail you need to provide useful content entails doing research on your ideal customer.

You can do this via a survey linked to one of your social media accounts or a blog. You could do it simply by asking your readers and friends what their questions are about a particular topic in your niche. People like to feel important and special, and they're usually quite happy to provide you with their input. Also, you can look at similar websites and/or fan pages, for example, or monitor Twitter lists related to your customers' needs and check out the questions people are asking in t hose forums.

With a little bit of creativity and ingenuity, you can pick up on a tremendous amount of information about your ideal customer and discover the very things people want in a brand like yours. Provide those things to them, and you'll have customers for years to come.

Conclusion

The quest for brand authenticity is really a quest to be real and to communicate this sense of being real with customers in a way that is compelling, relevant, and, above all, true. Authenticity is most effectively communicated to customers in the telling of stories. Brands that attempt to communicate information to consumers without the narrative of the story ultimately struggle to survive. Brands that thrive are those that have identified what makes them unique, what they truly believe in, what their customers believe in, and how to deliver that information in the form of a great story their customers want to believe.

CHAPTER 3

AUTHENTIC MARKETERS ARE SUCCESSFUL BECAUSE THEY ARE JUST LIKE YOU

"If people like you, they'll listen to you. But if they trust you, they'll do business with you."
—Zig Ziglar

In the not-so-distant past, it wasn't atypical for people to buy most of their food and other necessities from people they knew. Eggs were picked up from the farmer down the street, Mrs. Jones sewed (or at least mended) dresses, and kids went to school with the banker's kids.

Compare this to how most of our shopping is done today. You likely get most of your groceries and household supplies at a mega grocery store and take your mending to the dry cleaner at the mall. You probably don't even know your bank teller's name, never mind the name of the bank manager.

With more and more of us using the Internet to buy everything from food, to clothes, to jewelry and even cars, we are only going to see this chasm between seller and buyer increase.

Whereas we used to be able to see and even personally knew the person selling to us, more and more we are buying from nameless, faceless organizations, which know nothing about us.

So where does this leave us as marketers? How do we build trust and meaningful connections with people we may never even meet in real life? How do we communicate and live out this trust, particularly with more and more of our transactions being done online?

The long and short of it is that people buy from people, companies, and brands they know and trust. This means it is incumbent upon marketers not only to be worthy of this trust (trustworthy), but to find ways to display characteristics they know their target audience will embrace.

This is the bond that ultimately will translate into sales.

So how do you know what characteristics your customers value? How do you know what is important to them? As the foundational principle upon which your products, services, and marketing efforts are built, this is no small question.

Who Is Your Target Audience, and What Does It Value?

Identifying your target audience is a critical first step to creating an effective marketing message. Understanding and identifying with your customers' needs and pain points is not only critical when it comes to creating or designing a product, it is also essential for knowing *exactly how they want to be sold to.*

But how on earth do you figure out something as complex as marketing preferences? One way to approach this task is to narrow down the question by focusing on **values**.

Keep in mind that not all target audiences are equal, so their values won't be the same across the board. Customer values likely will vary by geographic area, niche, and demographic characteristics, such as gender, age, and marital status. But while your target audience won't share all the same values, there is likely to be a trend or leaning toward particular types of values.

For instance, if you run a store that sells musical instruments, your target market, generally speaking, may value community and creativity. Or if you sell specialized computer equipment, you may find your customers are generally detail-oriented, and value numbers, formulas, and data.

One company that is flourishing in large part due to its commitment to honoring its customers' values is outdoor clothing manufacturer and retailer Patagonia.

In what most would consider a risky move, it launched an ad campaign (on Cyber Monday, no less) advising its customers *not* to buy a jacket. Detailing the environmental impact of producing one of its top-selling jackets, it encouraged customers to "do the opposite of every other business today. We ask you to buy less and to reflect before you spend a dime on this jacket or anything else."

Patagonia has built a brand known for responsible and transparent manufacturing and sourcing, even showing customers a detailed account of the factories in which its clothing is made as well as the environmental impact of manufacturing the clothes.

To some, this may seem foolhardy. But Patagonia has managed to build a brand that speaks to the needs of those who want to be better, who want to make a difference in the world and to work toward a sustainable future.

Businesses like Patagonia know that honoring the values of their target market is a fundamental piece of their overall business strategy, from where they manufacture the product (locally or overseas), to how they manufacture it (sustainably or as inexpensively as possible), to how they market the product (more emphasis on online marketing versus offline). The importance of understanding your customers' values can't be overstated.

Ways to Identify What Your Target Market Values

Being at odds with your target market's values is a surefire recipe for disaster—both for your customers and for your business.

It would be a mistake to assume you know the values of your market without doing any objective research. While the title of this chapter is "Authentic Marketers Are Successful Because They Are Just Like You," this doesn't mean you should assume your customers want what you want, or that they have the same needs as you do.

Then how do you go about figuring out what's important to your customers? How do you come to know their beliefs, values, and pain points? Gathering this kind of complex intelligence will mean relying on a number of sources.

Trade Publications

Trade publications can be a great source of information. However, they are unlikely to tell you explicitly what the needs and values of your customers are. But by reading between the lines, you can gain a good deal of insight into customer behaviors, industry trends, and what types of products and brands in your industry are building positive relationships with their customers.

Focus Groups

Gather a group of people in your target audience, either online or in person, and ask the people what is important to them, what problems they are trying to solve, and what values they hold—not just in relation to your product or service. Find out what their interests are and what they like to do in their free time. Remember, their values influence every aspect of their lives. More importantly, from a marketing perspective, they influence how they buy!

One-on-One Interviews

Like focus groups, interviews will give you insight into the needs and values of your target market. However, sitting down and talking one-on-one with your "ideal" customer is a great way to dig even deeper into the values of your target market.

Social Media and Online Forums

Stepping back and observing what is being said about your brand and your industry in general can be a great way to get an insider's view on what's important to your target market. What complaints do people have about your industry? What needs are not being met? How can you address these concerns and values both within your product and in the way you market it?

Trends in Your Industry

Using tools like Google Trends and Google Alerts, look at what people in your target market are looking for and engaging with online. For instance, do people seem to increasingly value environmentally friendly products? Are low price points important to them? Is reliability currently lacking in your industry? By understanding what people are searching for online, you can better understand what is missing in the marketplace and work toward meeting this need. Ultimately, the goal is to provide solutions for your target market.

EXERCISE: DEFINING TARGET MARKET'S VALUES

If you are struggling to define the value set of your target market, take the next few minutes to jot down responses to these exercises:

1. List three demographic markers that are common for people in your target audience. Examples include age range, ethnicity, geographic location, income, and marital status.
2. Next, list three personal characteristics that this target audience commonly displays. Examples include being creative, technologically savvy, laid-back, and detail-oriented.
3. Brainstorm a few ways your business can potentially meet the needs of your customers in light of Nos. 1 and 2. How can your products, your services, and the ways you promote them speak to these characteristics? What values does this audience hold, and how can you honor these values in your business?

How to Build Trust on Social Media

Social media can be an extremely powerful tool for connecting with your customers or clients. Never before have marketers had such a privilege and opportunity to connect and build trust with current and potential customers. However, this opportunity comes with its own unique set of responsibilities.

Following are ways you can establish authentic relationships and build trust using social media.

Don't Be a Know-it-all

There are far too many "experts" on social media who cannot seem to stop talking about themselves. They constantly offer unsolicited advice, go on and on about their latest achievements, and generally seem to enjoy controlling the conversation.

It could be that they see this type of behavior as the best way to establish themselves as experts, and therefore portray themselves as trustworthy. However, what they are actually doing is alienating themselves from the people who are the very foundation of their business.

Instead of feeling like you always have to have all the answers, do not be afraid to admit you don't know something. If you don't have an answer, don't just fake it; promise to find out. *Your community would much rather see you as a regular person than as someone who thinks he or she knows everything.*

Provide True Value

Authentic marketers do not use social media to blow smoke; they use it to provide true value to their audience. In this age of content marketing, consumers are looking to connect with brands that generously provide unique, valuable content by way of social media updates, blog posts, email newsletters, webinars, and more.

Ask yourself: *What is the primary purpose of my content on social media? Is it to come across as an expert in my field? Is it to make sales or gain leads? Is it to attract search engine traffic? Or is it to genuinely make life easier for my customers?*

Ask Questions (and Listen to the Answers)

Social media was never intended as a replacement for traditional "interruption" marketing. Marketers who carry techniques traditionally used for creating television ads or billboards over to social media will be sorely disappointed with the results of their social media efforts.

Authentic marketers know the beauty of social media lies in the ***dialogue*** it allows between brands and their customers. Brands can ask questions, get feedback, and then incorporate that feedback into the creation of products, the way they market their goods, and the way they relate to their customers.

Reach Out to Others

While cliché, no man (or woman) is an island. This is particularly true on social media. Brands that use social media primarily to broadcast their message inevitably will end up feeling pretty lonely.

Using social media authentically, on the other hand, means reaching out to others in your niche, industry, or field. It means following your followers, and looking for new people to follow or "friend." It means learning from others, interacting through online conversations, and continually building new connections and relationships.

Don't just sit and wait for people to come to you. *Seek them out.* Make new friends and connections. Constantly be thinking about how you can help others. Be generous about sharing great information—give to get!

Express Your Passion (and Be Truly Passionate)

True passion cannot be faked. If you are passionate about what you do and about the people you serve, this will be evident in the way you interact in social media. The same is true of feigning passion in social media; it too is easy to spot and will be obvious to everyone around you. People can sniff out a fake in a heartbeat today.

Passionless marketing is fraught with problems, to say the least. While you may be able to get away with it in the short term, in the long run you will just end up alienating your customers and losing their trust.

Consistency and Reliability: The Glue That Holds Trust Together

If people ultimately buy from those they know and trust, how do businesses prove they are trustworthy? You can't fake trust, so what fundamental characteristics do brands need to display to earn this trust?

I would argue that the two foundational characteristics of brands that deserve and earn trust are *consistency* and *reliability*.

We all know brands that are full of hype; they say such things as:

"Limited quantities available!"
"We're slashing prices!"
"Lowest prices guaranteed!"

Now, don't get me wrong; these statements are not necessarily bad in and of themselves. However, oftentimes when these types of statements are made, they are not *backed up by reality.* I mean, in reality, do most businesses only have a limited quantity of product to sell? If they do, they can definitely feel good about using this in their marketing message. But if they are just saying it to get their customers to buy quickly, this is a great strategy for getting your customers to lose trust in you.

Trust Isn't Built Overnight

It is easy to be consistent with your customers once or twice. (Do you see the irony here?) It is far more difficult to be reliable on a continual basis. However, this is exactly what is needed to ultimately win the trust of your customers.

When people see that you are present and engaged on a continual basis, their trust in you slowly builds. Trust isn't something you can win through one great marketing campaign or promotion. Trust must be earned over time.

Think about someone—maybe a family member, friend, or neighbor—who only comes to you when he or she needs something. When you see this person's name on the call display, your stomach probably sinks because you know he or she wants something from you.

Marketers who only communicate and engage with their community when they want something will quickly earn the same reputation. Instead of their fans or followers looking forward to their updates or tweets, they'll begin to dread them. ("Oh, no—is he trying to sell me something again?")

But when people get the sense that you care about them, listen to them, and want to be part of their world, their trust in you will begin to grow. This is when bonds begin to form, relationships form, and community begins to grow.

Being reliable does not mean never making mistakes. We all make mistakes from time to time; that is part of life. However, being reliable *does* mean acknowledging when you make mistakes and promising to do better next time. It means being transparent and being the type of person and business that is worthy of trust. People do not mind if you screw up, but they do mind if you don't fix it! Own your mistakes, and your audience will love you for it.

How to Become a Trusted Advisor to Your Community

We all know that to gain trust, you must be trustworthy. But what does this mean in practice? If you are passionate about what you are promoting and about the people you serve, how do you convey this passion to your community?

Communicate in Language They Know and Are Comfortable With

When you communicate with your community, are you speaking in a way they understand? Are you using their language? Can they relate to the examples and analogies you're using? Are you using slang or industry jargon when you communicate with them?

Through understanding your target market, you will get a better sense of how they prefer to communicate. Do they tend to be highly educated? Then you may want to avoid using too much slang. Are they laid-back and informal? Then they may appreciate real-world examples and a more casual dialogue.

Center Content Around Topics That Interest Them

Just because your competitors are creating content around a certain topic does not necessarily mean that is best for your community. Figure out the needs and desires of *your* unique community by asking yourself:

- *What questions are they asking on social media?*
- *What common concerns are cropping up in my blog comments?*
- *What issues or problems are they telling me they face?*

Do not create content based solely on your suspicions about what people want to see. Pay close attention to which blog posts are gaining traction and getting a lot of attention. Note which Pinterest images are getting loads of re-pins in your community. Which Facebook posts are getting liked and shared by your fans? What tweets are getting retweeted on Twitter?

Create content that you know your community is interested in and that is useful to them. Their trust in you inevitably will grow. As they come to sense that you truly understand their needs and interests, you will become top of mind for them when they need your product or service.

Consistently Provide Value

We have talked about the importance of being consistent and reliable. One of the best ways you can demonstrate these characteristics is by continually providing value to your community.

There are many ways you can provide value:

- By consistently offering helpful, unique content.
- By offering webinars or podcasts.

- By keeping your community informed about the goings-on in your industry.
- By taking time to answer questions posted on social media.
- By offering amazing customer service.

There are almost limitless ways you can provide value to your community. The core question you should be asking yourself is, *What do my customers need, and how can I provide that?* If you can meet these needs, you are, by definition, providing value and are well on your way to gaining their trust.

Be Passionate About Things They Are Passionate About

True passion is contagious. Make a point of really listening to what your customers are talking about, both offline and online. I am not just talking about things related to your business!

These people on the other side of your computer screen are real people, with real lives and interests besides your product or brand (hard to believe, I know). Don't be afraid to engage with your customers about hobbies, interests, or topics that are not related to your business. People will connect with you on a personal level before they connect with you on a business level.

Are your customers sports fanatics? Do they tend to gravitate toward classical music? Do they eagerly await the next Apple product launch? Ask them about their

passions. *Authentic marketers get excited about the things their community is passionate about.*

When you take the time and effort to truly understand the needs and values of your customers, great things start to happen. Your products, services, and marketing strategies begin to develop organically because everything is done with the customers' needs in mind. Your presence in social media naturally becomes more about building connections and providing value, and less about generating leads or making sales.

When you consistently act in trustworthy ways, those in your community begin to have faith in you and to understand that you care about them and their needs. It is *this* relationship that invariably will lead to long-term, authentic, profitable relationships.

Chapter 4

AUTHENTIC MARKETERS ARE PASSIONATE

"Do what you love, and the money will follow."
—Marsha Sinetar

You may have heard of Tony Hsieh, founder and CEO of one of the largest shoe retailers on the web. If you haven't, likely you have at least heard of his company, Zappos. It is renowned for its fun-loving company culture, family-centered values, legendary customer service, and the passion and determination of its leaders and employees.

But something you may not know is that Tony, while passionate about his company, is not necessarily passionate about shoes. This hasn't stopped him, however, from building a wildly successful shoe empire based on something that *is* his true passion: *customer service.* In Tony's words, according to multiple Internet sources, "We asked ourselves what we wanted this company to stand for. We didn't want to just sell shoes. I wasn't even into shoes—but I was passionate about customer service."

In nine years, Tony took Zappos from a penny-pinching startup to a multibillion-dollar powerhouse. By focusing on building a company culture in which passion for serving others was foundational, superb customer service has grown to become the defining characteristic of a company that easily could have been known for just selling shoes.

Why Passion Matters, and Why It Makes You a More Authentic Marketer

Entrepreneurs like Tony Hsieh know that aligning your business and your passion is critical to being a truly authentic marketer. When you believe in something and are passionate about it, you can't help but tell others. Your message is authentic because it is a natural outpouring of what you believe, not something forced or contrived. On the other hand, a marketer who doesn't feel passionate about what he is doing can say all the right words, but not with any real degree of authenticity.

Saying that passion is necessary for authenticity may sound somewhat like a platitude, but in a number of concrete ways, passion directly leads to authenticity in marketing. Here are just a few:

Passion Serves as a Compass to Maintain Authenticity

Think of passion as a compass used in maintaining authenticity. When you no longer feel passionate about what you are doing, it is difficult—or, I would argue, even impossible—to be an authentic marketer. It is at this point (or ideally even before) that you need to figure out where this lack of passion is coming from.

Many marketers experience a loss of passion for their work at one time or another, and contrary as it may seem, this isn't always a bad thing. Recognizing a lack of passion can be a red flag that something is amiss in your professional or personal life. This realization may be just the push you need to figure out what is wrong and then to work at fixing it.

Passion also can serve as a compass in your day-to-day decision-making and interpersonal dealings. If you find yourself feeling ambivalent about a decision you have made, it may be worth examining how it fits with or contradicts your beliefs and passions.

Passion Drives Action

To put it simply, authentic passion *energizes*. When you feel passionate, you almost can't help but take action. It becomes a natural outpouring of what you believe in and what you feel you must do. It is what ***drives*** you.

Have you ever lain awake in bed at night with ideas swimming around in your head? Have you ever been so excited about an idea, project, or event that you could literally feel the electricity running through your arms and legs? This is what true passion does. It spurs you on, giving you energy to do what needs to get done. When passion aligns with work, you will find you *gain* energy rather than lose it. This isn't to say you will never get tired! But it does mean you will start to find you take action as a natural result of your passion. Rather than carrying out tasks because you have to, you will find yourself doing them with joy.

Passion Carries You Through When Times Get Tough

Marketers who are passionate about what they do (like Tony) experience a deep satisfaction in their work and can rely on their passion as an anchor when facing difficult circumstances. Passion acts as a sustaining force when challenging circumstances transpire.

Just like extroverts gain energy by being around other people, passion acts as a fuel source, especially when things are not going your way. Passion is what will get you out of bed those mornings when you ask yourself *why* you do what you do. When it feels like the world is against you, a true passion and love for what you do and, more importantly, for the people you serve will be the force that sustains you and keeps you moving forward.

Being Passionate About Something Makes You Feel Good

There is no doubt about it—passion feels amazing. Think about how you feel when you are doing something you truly love. Whether that is fishing, hiking on a beautiful summer day, or having a romantic night out with your spouse, it certainly doesn't feel like a task. You feel energized, happy, and content.

When you are able to align your work with your passion, you get to experience these feelings not just when you are participating in a favorite activity or hobby, but throughout all aspects of your life. When you feel a deep sense of connection to what you are doing, your work becomes more than just *work*. If you truly enjoy what you are doing, it doesn't feel like *work* at all.

Your Passion Influences Those Around You

When was the last time you were *really* excited about something? Maybe you got a sparkling new car, landed a first-rate client, or got a new dog. What behaviors did you exhibit after you got the good news?

Chances are you couldn't wait to tell the world. You likely emailed your friends, called your mom, and just *happened* to casually pepper all your conversations with mentions of this latest development. You were bursting with happiness and the pride of achievement, and you couldn't wait to share your excitement with everyone around you. ***This is the very definition of an authentic message***.

This message and the genuine enthusiasm with which you spread it organically inspires and influences those around you. Instead of coming up with strategies to inspire your employees, for instance, a natural consequence of passion is that they will want to experience the same passion they see in you.

The Difference Between Hype and Passion

Tony Hsieh's enthusiasm and dedication to customer service is a great example of true passion. His passion comes from his deep-rooted beliefs, values, and the sincere desire to do what he feels is right. Hype, on the other hand, in some ways could be defined as the lack of passion, or even as a form of inauthentic passion. Although some of the outward characteristics of hype and passion are similar, one is authentic and sustainable, and one isn't. (Can you guess which is which?)

So how do you know if what you are experiencing is true passion or just hype?

To give you an example of hype, think about how car companies tend to advertise: enthusiastically, using such phrases as "Come on down" and "Biggest sale ever" on garish yellow signs. How do you feel when you are marketed to in this way? Do you feel the car dealership understands your needs and pain points? Do you feel it has a deep-seated desire to help you?

Passion, on the other hand, is primarily about the ***other***. It's not rooted in selfish gains or desires, but instead constantly looks for ways to make life easier for others. Unlike hype, it cannot be faked. Passion is authentic and sustainable, while hype is short-lived and fragile.

EXERCISE: FINDING YOUR PASSION

Finding your passion can be difficult. It can be easy to assume everyone around you knows what he wants out of life and can articulate what drives him and gives his life meaning.

One way to figure out what activities or goals will be most likely to give you passion and energy is to think about how you respond to various situations in your personal and professional life. Take a few minutes to answer the following questions to see how well your work and passion align.

- What activities do you take part in that make you feel "alive"?
- What motivates you in your work?
- Does your personality type work well with the type of work you're doing?
- Are you more focused on completing tasks or on helping others?
- What aspect of your job makes you feel the most inspired and excited?
- Think about a time when you felt passionate about your work. What was different then?
- Are your passion and your work aligned? If not, is there anything you can do to make this happen?

The Effects of Passionless Marketing

So, why does all this matter? As long as you are saying all the right things, isn't that enough? I mean, people can't exactly read your mind, right?

Wrong (well, kind of).

While they may not be able to read your mind, people, even if only subconsciously, are increasingly looking to weed out the snake oil salesmen. As mentioned in an earlier chapter, in a world where honesty and integrity are at a premium, consumers are getting better at spotting false excitement and false passion.

So what are the effects of passionless, inauthentic marketing? Who does it really hurt?

Passionless Marketing Leads to Personal and Professional Burnout

Marketers who continually push a message they aren't passionate about are likely to experience personal and professional burnout. When day after day you promote something you don't believe in, or promote it in a way you are not comfortable with, you not only lose your day-to-day enjoyment of life, but inevitably will experience some degree of burnout.

Any introverts reading this? Think about how you feel when you have been with people all day. Likely you feel tired, restless, and maybe even irritable. A key trait of introversion is that being alone gives energy, while being with people takes it away.

The same is true for promoting something you are not passionate about. Feigning excitement sucks your energy, leaving you tired and irritable. You may even come to resent your customers or others in your organization, as you may feel they are somehow responsible for your feelings of irritability.

But when you are promoting something you truly believe in, something you are passionate about and want to tell the world about—this *gives* you energy. It inspires you to freely share your message with others.

Passionless Marketing Means Having to Remember Your Lies

As an example of a sentiment I am seeing more and more in marketing, here is an online excerpt referring to the role of lying in social media:

> *This is true for all social media. Lie, and lie a lot. Just make sure that you do not contradict yourself, and make sure your lies cannot be easily disproved. For example, claiming you are the president of IBM is going to be easy to disprove, but saying that you attended Harvard is not. What are they going to do, look through all the Harvard registrations for your name?*

While most marketers don't participate in any type of blatant lying (or at least wouldn't admit to it!), promoting a product, service, or business you don't believe in does mean having to keep track of what you have said and what you *should* say. When you don't care one way or the other about what you are promoting, you tend to recite a script, say all the "right" things, and hope for the best.

When you truly believe in what you are promoting, your message is consistent and comes easily and naturally. There is no having to remember what you may have said or what you should say next. You just say what you think, what you feel, and what you know to be true.

Passionless Marketing Means Losing Trust

Passionless marketing doesn't just impact the marketer himself or herself. As mentioned, in a world of increasingly inauthentic marketing, consumers are more and more aware of inconsistencies in your story. If they get any sense that what you are saying may not be entirely true, they are outta there.

I am not just talking about when it comes to marketing a subpar product. Your product may be worthy of accolades, may be the greatest invention of the year, in fact, but if you don't *believe in it,* it's going to be pretty hard to feel passionate about it and even harder to project that passion. And this lack of passion is going to be obvious to everyone around you: to your customers, to your employees, to everyone with whom you come into contact.

When those around you begin to sense that you are not truly passionate about what you are promoting, their level of trust in you will begin to diminish quickly. Trust isn't easily regained, so I am sure you can see why it is important to avoid passionless marketing at all costs.

How to Leverage Passion in Your Social Media Marketing

As mentioned, if you are truly passionate about something, those around you can't help but notice. In social media, the effects of your deep-rooted enthusiasm can be exponentially bigger than in "real life." Your passion can be expressed to hundreds or thousands of people at the same time, and because passion tends to be contagious, those people can continue to spread your enthusiasm to others. Excitement is truly contagious!

So, how do you leverage your passion within the context of your social media marketing?

1. Express your passion.

Of course, sharing your passion with others is a critical element of social media marketing. Traditional marketing methods have a more difficult time with this one. For instance, how would one share passion with consumers via a billboard, magazine ad, or TV commercial? All these methods are far more about pushing a message than about expressing passion.

Social media marketing, on the other hand, allows for passionate two-way discourse. Marketers have the opportunity to share their passion, but then others can respond and contribute to the discussion. Both parties are able to express their passion and feed off the energy of the other.

Don't be afraid to express your excitement or enthusiasm on social media. Passion is infectious, and it inspires others to want to be part of what you are doing. It excites and motivates others to share the good news as brand advocates.

2. Participate in the passion of others.

To assume that sharing your passion with your fans or followers via social media is your one and only goal in terms of marketing would be a big mistake. Regardless of your niche, there will be people who are excited, enthusiastic, and passionate about your industry, your business, or your product.

So while *your* passion is an essential component of connecting with your customers on social media, tapping into *their passion* is also critical.

Erich Marx, director of interactive and social media for automotive manufacturer Nissan, believes brands need to be intentional about participating in this existing passion:

> *There's an unbelievable amount of passion regarding the industry and cars. So, it's a natural fit. Whether Nissan or anyone else participates, there are conversations and articles being written and blogs. There's so much passion and energy about cars from consumers. We want to be a participant in the passion.*

A key way you can participate in the passion of your fans is by listening to and responding to positive comments. We know the importance of promptly responding to customer complaints on social media, but are we as quick to respond to positive remarks left on our blogs or Facebook pages?

Respond to compliments or kudos with the same fervor you would to complaints. Thank people for taking time to comment. Participate in lighthearted discussions simply to participate in your shared passion.

3. Leverage the passion of your social advocates.

A customer is someone who has bought your product or service. A social advocate is someone who is highly satisfied with your product or service, and who promotes your business online out of a deep sense of loyalty and affinity for your brand. These social advocates spread the word about your business through word of mouth, and because they are more likely to understand your brand's core values, they are highly effective external marketing machines.

These so-called "superfans" can increase your reach exponentially, so investing time and energy in identifying and encouraging them is more than worth your while. As a natural effect of their passion for your brand or product, they may:

- Write blog posts about your products.
- Recommend your brand to friends and family.

- Mention your brand on social media.
- Participate in forum discussions about your brand.
- Review or rate your products on shopping sites.

Typically, brand advocates do not ask for or need external incentives to promote your brand. It is because of their passion for your product or company that they are enthusiastically spreading the good news. However, these superfans also may have a deep desire to engage with your brand. This means it is important for brands not only to identify their advocates, but to nurture these relationships by showing appreciation for their support.

4. Inspire your employees with your passion.

Passion is easy to spot. True passion is hard to suppress and tends to ooze out in your day-to-day dealings, whether you know it or not. When you are passionate about what you are doing, this passion can't help but rub off on those around you.

As the first face of your business, it is critical that your employees be passionate about what they do. However, your employees will never have the same vested interest in your business or product as you do. This is why it is so important that *your* passion inspire *theirs.* Encourage your employees to share and be a part of the vision you have for your brand. People love to be part of something bigger than themselves!

Why do you love what you do? What excites you about your work? What meaning does it bring to your life? Share these insights with your employees, and watch the spark of passion begin to grow in them. I guarantee that when people at *all* levels of your organization begin to share a vision and a passion, great things will start to happen.

5. Tie your passion to business-related outcomes.

Have you heard the saying, "Do what you love, and you never work a day in your life"? That is the corollary to the quote at the beginning of this chapter, "Do what you love, and the money will follow." There is a caveat that ties these two sayings together, though: You must create a money-making business venture that is centered around what you are truly passionate about.

Let's take Tony Hsieh as an example. Remember, Tony was passionate about customer service, not shoes. He simply found a great vehicle for channeling that passion into a profitable business venture. What if Tony had instead channeled his insatiable passion for customer service into something far less lucrative? What if Tony instead had taken a low-paying job as a customer service agent in a call center? His passion for customer service would have been satisfied, and he may have even loved his job, but the financial results for Tony personally would have been much different.

So what is the moral to this story? Once you find out what you are truly passionate about, find a way to incorporate it as profitably as possible into your business model. Not only will exercising that passion make you love what you do more, but it also will add dramatically to your bottom line.

Conclusion

Let me ask you a question: Do you go to bed at night looking forward to work the next day, or do you experience a sense of apprehension or even dread at the prospect of having to "do it all over again"?

If you look forward to work, there's a good chance your work and your passion are aligned. When you do what you love and believe in, you will feel hopeful and energized, and you can rest assured that you are conducting your business in an authentic way. But if your work starts to become primarily about making money, gaining recognition, or any other self-serving purpose, I can guarantee your passion will start to dwindle. *These motivations will not be enough to sustain you long term.*

What do you want to define you and your business? What do you want people to remember about your business ten years from now? *This* is your passion. Run with it.

Chapter 5

AUTHENTIC MARKETERS DON'T CONTROL THE CONVERSATION

"As you know by now, people are talking about you. Wouldn't you rather have them talking with you?"
—**Andy Sernovitz**, Word of Mouth Marketing

Do you know what people are saying about your brand online? If you are having a hard time coming up with an answer, it may be time to take a fresh look at the way you are using social media for your business.

In the early days of social media, brands struggled with shifting their marketing tactics from traditional "push" methods to more conversational "pull" methods. Many times, companies would simply carry over their old strategies and techniques, using social media to broadcast their message to their audience. Would it surprise you to know this wasn't exactly a resounding success?

Smart brands know that in this new age of marketing, far more is happening than just a shift in the channel of delivery of their marketing message. Social media isn't simply a more convenient method of reaching large numbers of consumers with their message. It is not just an "add-on" to old, outbound methods of marketing.

Rather, it is a radical shift in the fundamental principles of marketing, the way people communicate, and, most importantly, the way they buy. The old ways simply don't work anymore.

To help explain, it would be helpful to take a trip back in time to see just how far marketing has come over the years and how, in some ways, we are coming full circle, back to our roots.

The Early Days of Marketing

In the "old days," everything was sold via word of mouth. The success or failure of your business depended almost entirely on what people were saying about you and your products. In a limited marketplace, where a village may only have a few merchants selling a particular product, the stories people were telling about your business and products mattered immensely.

"I hear Clodius offers the best price on leather. He's a full two denarii cheaper than that Flavius down the road!"

"Augustine ripped me off! He sold me stale spices and won't give me my money back. Don't buy from him!"

Successful merchants knew they had to have a great product and that their livelihood depended on what people were saying about their products and the way they ran their business. They typically succeeded not only because they had a high-quality product or service, but because they were forced to deal with their customers face to face. By "forced," I mean if something went wrong, they had to fix it or run the risk of everybody knowing they did not. Since you had no choice but to be accountable, it made sense to deal with any problems early, before your reputation could be damaged.

This early word-of-mouth marketing was instrumental in whether a business would survive and flourish. If your customers liked what you were doing, you hoped they would tell their neighbors and family members. If you were really lucky, these neighbors would come buy your goods. What people knew about your business was largely what they heard from others; in other words, **consumers controlled the conversation**.

Based solely on word of mouth, you could build the biggest, most profitable business in your village. Although it might have taken twenty years to earn the reputation of being the "best corn supplier in the valley," once you had earned it, you didn't need to worry that your business would fail.

A Shift to Brand-Controlled Marketing

Fast forward to the communication age. In previous generations, the quality, availability, and convenience of a business's products, along with how it treated its customers, was paramount to the success of a business. Now, however, brands had the ability not only to custom design their own marketing message, but to broadcast it to the masses.

With the invention of the first motor vehicle around the turn of the twentieth century, the world suddenly became far smaller. If your local store didn't have a product you needed, you now had the option of traveling to a neighboring city with relative ease. Products were easier to ship, and consumers had far more brand choices.

With the emergence of radio and television, marketing experienced an even greater shift; for the first time, companies could easily reach a massive group of consumers, both in person and now via the airwaves. They not only could craft their own message, but could broadcast it directly into people's homes. This was the beginning of what we now call "push marketing."

Research told us that "impressions" were what mattered. Reaching the greatest number of people was the goal. Advertising via billboards, and newspaper, TV, and radio ads meant being able to broadcast your marketing message to hundreds of thousands or even millions of people.

As long as you had a budget big enough to buy impressions, you were set. The company that had the biggest budget won. Big companies thrived because they had the budgets to dominate the game and because consumers had few channels to object or form a collective opinion. **Brands controlled the conversation.**

Coming Full Circle: Brands Participate in the Conversation

Finally, here we are in the Internet age. Whereas brands were able to control their own message just a decade or so ago, now they are increasingly becoming observers of and participants in conversations taking place by consumers.

With TV commercials being recorded on DVRs and skipped, and traditional print newspapers being all but dead, brands are rapidly losing the ability to determine in which direction the conversation is going to go. Instead of marketing departments carefully crafting messages and "pushing" these messages onto potential customers, consumers are gaining back power as their voices can be heard (and actually matter!) on social media.

In other words, "push" advertising has turned into "pull" advertising. To be successful, companies now need to ***attract*** their prospects, not blast them to death with impressions. Rather than broadcasting a message, they need to listen to the conversation already taking place.

For the first time, customers can talk back in massive quantities using social media. If they are dissatisfied with your product or unhappy with your customer service, they can simply tweet their displeasure using your company username or a hashtag, broadcasting

their complaint to thousands of people at once. They can make their voice heard and form collective opinions about your product or business. Again, **consumers control the conversation**.

In the digital age, word-of-mouth marketing is back in full force. In fact, we are seeing brand reputations—once made or lost over the course of decades or even generations—being built or destroyed seemingly in an instant. Smart brands are the ones that acknowledge this massive shift and use it to their advantage.

How You Can Participate in the Conversation

So how can businesses be part of this conversation that is happening about their brand? When is it time to respond, as opposed to just listening? What is the best way to take part in the conversation, without trying to control it?

Be Where Your Community Is Talking

Fashion retailer H&M knows that a key component of a solid social media strategy is being where your customers are. Their stated goal behind using Google+ is to "be where our customers are, have a dialogue, and share the latest fashion."

While they make a point of posting new content daily, they are also careful to participate and engage with what their followers are posting. They share their followers' contributions with their community, participate in

conversations started by their followers, and, in so doing, are rapidly expanding their reach.

As H&M already has discovered, to participate in the conversations taking place about your business, you first need to know where your target market is "hanging out." Depending on your niche, your customers may tend to be spread out evenly over many channels, or they may primarily be making use of just one or two.

The important thing is you figure out *where the conversation is taking place.* If you are not active and available to your customers where they prefer to be, you can bet your competitors will be!

To figure out where your community is talking, start by reviewing the demographic data of social networks. For instance, did you know Pinterest users tend to be female, have some level of college education, and have an annual household income of $100,000-plus? Or that Tumblr draws some of the youngest users among all social media sites, with 45 percent under age thirty-five?

As we discussed, knowing what your customers value is paramount to knowing how to meet their needs. This knowledge is also important for figuring out what social networks will most appeal to them. For instance, if your customers are service-related businesses, they are more likely to be active and engaged on LinkedIn. If they are more creative and artistic, they are more likely to use visually centric platforms, such as Pinterest.

Be where your community is talking, and never risk being left out of the conversation!

How Do You Hear the Conversation?

Simply setting up profiles where your customers are talking will not be enough to hear the conversations. Businesses need to be proactive about listening to discussions, and this isn't always an obvious process.

So, how do you go about "listening in" on conversations taking place? How do you figure out what people are saying about your brand? Here are two ways you can hear the conversation:

Use Filters to Find Out What's Being Said

Filters are any tools that allow you to sift through the reams of content being produced and broadcast on social media. One of the most popular examples of social media filters is *hashtags*. As every major social networking site allows the use of hashtags, they can be a great way of finding out what people are saying about your business, products, or industry.

By tracking conversations that are happening about your industry (for instance, an author may follow #WritingTip), as well as conversations about your brand (like #Ford or #Cocacola), you can make sure you always know what people are saying.

Another way to filter content is through on-site searches. With the recent changes being made to Facebook Graph Search, finding out what people are saying about your brand is becoming even easier. For instance, try running a query for "posts about ______" (inserting your

brand name or a topic related to your industry). This can be a great way to view public posts related to your brand or industry.

Use Facebook Interest Lists, Twitter Lists, and Google Circles

With so many free and inexpensive tools available to help you stay on top of the conversation, there is no reason to feel overwhelmed by the task. The top three social media sites have ways for you to organize real-time "conversations."

Each of the major social networks allows you to segment content into different categories. While social media can be quite easy to monitor when you only have a few friends or followers, it can quickly become slightly chaotic as your influence and your audience build on the various social platforms.

Facebook interest lists are a great way to cut through the clutter and see only the most important conversations about your brand or industry. For instance, by creating a list of top influencers in your industry, you can always be on top of the latest news and topics of interest to your community.

In the same way, Twitter lists and Google circles allow users to segment the people they follow. Segmenting in this way ensures you don't miss out on important trends or conversations involving influencers in your industry, your competitors, customers, or your target market.

What Is Reputation Management? (It's *always* better to know!)

Say what you want about Walmart, but it is making great strides when it comes to participating in the conversation taking place about the company online. Until recently, Walmart typically chose not to respond to negative tweets mentioning its brand. While the company was present where its customers were talking about it (Twitter), it was allowing the conversation to take place without it.

The company's social media strategy was largely aimed at pushing its message to its fans and followers. In other words, it was trying to **control the conversation**. While Walmart knew its customers were talking about its brand, it chose to largely ignore the conversation in favor of carrying on with its own.

However, recently Walmart decided to implement a radical shift in how it handled criticisms and complaints on Twitter. Using the mantra "no free shots," the company is now taking a much more active approach to handling complaints.

Chad Mitchell, Walmart's senior director of digital communications, says, on the site Digiday, that the company is realizing the value of dialogue over pushing a message:

> *Best case scenario, we're able to engage, share some content, and change hearts and minds. Worst case, we're able to have an open dialogue and then move on, agreeing to disagree.*

Walmart is learning that regardless of what people are saying about its brand, *it's better to know.* This is a good lesson for all marketers: People will be having the conversation with or without you, so why not let your voice be heard?

So how does social media play into this? What does it specifically involve? If reputation management is simply listening to and influencing conversations about your brand, what tasks do marketers need to focus on?

Listening and Monitoring

First and foremost, it involves listening to what is already being said. It means not jumping in without knowing the landscape or the general climate of the conversation. Using the tools mentioned, it means listening to what your customers (and potential customers) are saying about your brand and your industry.

What concerns do they have about your product? What are the pain points of your target market? What need isn't being met in the marketplace? It's only by actively listening to the conversation that you can get a good grasp on what's truly being said.

Active listening also means keeping track of what is being said. This means monitoring brand mentions, mentions of your competitors, as well as topics of interest in your industry. This not only will allow you to better understand your customers, but it will enable you to quickly identify any issues you need to address.

Responding Quickly

Not every comment will necessitate a response. However, being able to properly evaluate which ones need attention is of the utmost importance. For instance, did you know research suggests that 32 percent of customers who use social media expect a response within thirty minutes? And that 42 percent more expect a response within an hour? That's a lot of pressure on businesses!

Keep in mind that for every minute you don't respond to a customer comment (especially complaints!), that is one more minute he or she could be telling someone else. By responding quickly, you can decrease the chances that negative word of mouth will spread and increase the chances of resolving matters quickly and efficiently, thereby reducing much of the potential fallout.

Responding Consistently

For consistency's sake, I would encourage all businesses that are active on social media to have a plan in place for how they will respond to comments. For instance:

- Which types of comments will we respond to? Just customer service queries? Just criticisms? Just positive comments? All of the above?
- How quickly will we respond? Within one hour? Twenty-four hours? Three business days?
- Will we be responding as our brand or as individuals?

- What voice and values will we convey through our responses?
- Will we share or retweet positive comments?

These are all important questions to consider to achieve consistency for your brand.

How to Start the Conversation

While it's important to listen and respond to existing conversations, remember that your customers also want to hear from *you!* But how do you go about starting a conversation? And how do you elicit engagement from your community?

In chapter 5, I went over five ways brands can build trust on social media. It is these very strategies that will allow you to start conversations without coming across as someone who only cares about pushing his or her own message. Remember, *how* you share something on social media is just as important as *what* you share.

To briefly recap, here are the five ways to build trust on social media, as well as how they apply to "starting the conversation":

- **Don't be a know-it-all.** When you start a new conversation on social media, remember to approach it with a sense of collaboration and humility. Your opinion is not the be-all and end-all, even if you did start the conversation!

- **Provide true value.** Ask yourself, *Is my main goal to solve a problem, meet a need, or otherwise help the community?* If your answer is no, you may not be providing true value to your community.
- **Ask questions.** Conversation is a two-way street. Ask those in your community what is important to them, what they think about certain topics, and what you can do to improve your products or services.
- **Reach out to others.** Reaching out to others in your niche or industry and having them join in the conversation is a wonderful way to add a richer dimension to the discussion.
- **Express your passion.** Passion is contagious, so don't be afraid to let your enthusiasm show! As long as it is authentic excitement and not just hype (see chapter 6), you can't go wrong!

What to Do When the Conversation Doesn't Go as Planned

As is inevitable in most aspects of real life, there will come a time when something doesn't go according to plan. Try as you may, eventually there will be a conversation that doesn't go in the direction you would like, and with the speed and sheer reach of social media, one "small" problem can spread like wildfire.

That doesn't mean, however, that you are helpless, or that the situation is totally out of your control. By managing crises in a logical, strategic way, you can avoid much of the fallout that could otherwise occur.

Have a Plan in Advance

Earlier in this chapter, I talked about the importance of having a plan in terms of responding to comments on social media. It is equally important to have a plan for how to respond when problems arise.

By anticipating what challenges you may face on social media, you can carefully plan out your response calmly and efficiently. It is important to consider best- and worst-case scenarios, what your response would be in each instance, and who is responsible for overseeing each scenario (more on this follows).

For instance, do you recall hearing how ChapStick responded to negative remarks on its Facebook page a couple of years ago? After posting a risqué photo of a woman bending over a couch, looking for her ChapStick, the brand began receiving negative feedback from its community. ChapStick's response? Delete, delete, delete. As you might imagine, this didn't go over very well. Rather than responding to comments, it tried to silence its community and control the conversation.

Undoubtedly, had the company had a plan in place for dealing with such situations, it could have avoided much of the fallout.

Assign Responsibilities

When heated situations arise, it is critical to have a person or team in place that is qualified and prepared to deal with them. If there is no clear assignment of responsibilities, several unfortunate things could happen:

- Without a clear mandate to take responsibility for a situation, the most logical person may never step up to the plate. For instance, don't assume your social media manager knows he or she is responsible in crisis situations; make it clear to everyone involved.
- In crisis situations, tempers tend to flare and conflict may arise among team members. This can distract from dealing with the problem at hand.
- Everyone assuming someone else is handling it may lead to a diffusion of responsibility among team members.
- You also could have an escalation policy. In other words, if a team member cannot handle a situation, it gets bumped up to the social media manager. If that manager cannot handle it, a company official with more authority is contacted for a more formal response.

Respond Quickly

The speed at which you respond to comments is of the utmost importance. If customers are expecting a response within thirty minutes, that doesn't give you much time to think or breathe before you react!

In times of crisis, a quick and well-planned response is even more necessary. Don't give the situation time to get out of control. Don't give it time to take on a life of its own. The longer it takes to resolve the situation, the more opportunity there is for negative word of mouth to spread. Respond quickly, and you stand the best chance of showing your community you care and that you take their problems and concerns seriously.

EXERCISE: WHAT ARE PEOPLE SAYING ABOUT YOUR BRAND?

It is never too late to find out what people are saying about your brand. Take a few minutes to work through these steps to find out where your customers are, what they're saying about you, and how you can participate in the conversation:

- Identify the three social media sites most used by your online community.
- Use filters, tools, and site-specific features (interest lists, searches, circles, and so on) to find and follow fifteen to twenty comments, posts, or conversations involving your product, service, or brand.
- Ask yourself, *What is the general sentiment of the conversations?*

- Identify ways that being involved in the conversation would have benefited your company or brand.
- What procedures or policies could you implement to systematically be involved in future conversations?

Conversations about your brand are going to happen. The question is, do you want them to happen without you, or would you prefer to have your voice heard?

Although finding and contributing to these discussions is relatively simple, it does require a commitment to proactively listen to and monitor them. Responding in consistent, authentic ways will go a long way toward ensuring you are never left out of the conversation again.

CHAPTER 6

AUTHENTIC MARKETERS CONNECT WITH AND BUILD COMMUNITIES

"Community: A feeling of fellowship with others, as a result of sharing common attitudes, interests, and goals."

—Google

In 2009, Ford Motor Company set out to do something that had never been done in North America. In an attempt to raise great awareness about its newly launched Fiesta, Ford leveraged the enthusiasm and social influence of one hundred social "agents" to spread the word about the car across various social media channels.

It was a risky proposition, to be sure. Ford gave these twenty-something-year-old agents a Fiesta to use for free (gas and insurance included!) for six months. All Ford asked for in return was that they use social media to document their experience. Apart from giving broad guidance by way of assigning monthly "missions," the conversation was in the hands of the community.

Critics wondered: *Will these agents, when left to tell their own stories, generate positive buzz for the company? And will all this buzz translate into increased sales?*

The results were astounding. At the end of the six-month campaign, Ford had 6.2 million YouTube views, 750,000-plus Flickr views, nearly 4 million Twitter impressions, and, most importantly, ***50,000 interested potential customers.***

So, how was Ford able to leverage the influence of these agents with such success? What underlying factors were in place to support this bold initiative?

The 2009 Ford Fiesta Movement Campaign Attracted 50,000 Interested Potential Customers

As I see it, four main factors contributed to the success of the Ford Fiesta Movement:

1. Ford built a committed community around common interests.

The hundred agents, carefully chosen from a pool of four-thousand-plus applicants, were brought together at the outset of the campaign to hear all about it, the monthly missions, and the car. More importantly, they were allowed to meet one another, share their excitement, and create a community dynamic. The feeling was they were a united team, and they were in this important and fascinating adventure together.

So what characteristics did this group share? Most were young, had some degree of online influence, were Ford supporters, and, most importantly, were adventuresome by nature. According to Jeff Eggen, experiential marketing manager at Ford, their enthusiasm for adventure was immediately obvious:

> *When they got their Fiesta, it was sort of like the agents were winners on The Price Is Right, they were so excited! And since they are so into capturing their life experiences, many agents immediately started sending Twitter messages and live-streaming footage of themselves with the Fiesta.*

Ford knew that bringing together a group of like-minded individuals and giving them the opportunity to engage in activities they were excited about ultimately would lead to increased buzz about its brand.

2. Ford focused on a feeling of belonging and community, not just on a product or company.

Ford knew simply creating a conversation or marketing message aimed at the Fiesta's features or benefits wasn't going to cut it. The agents were carefully selected, in large part because they already had shown the ability to build significant communities of their own using social media.

This is where the monthly missions came in. Instead of simply touting the features of the Fiesta (for example, the rain-sensing windshield wipers), the company focused on bringing together the movement's community to enjoy a sense of collective adventure.

The agents brought their communities together to participate in the excitement of these monthly missions and in doing so, created a collective sense of adventure and intrigue. This was about far more than just a car; it was the *feeling of adventure* you could experience when you drove the car. It was all about telling a story to which others could relate!

3. Ford provided an outlet to support individuality.

It is important to note that Ford did not dictate what its agents should do or say in relation to the campaign. Though the company assigned them missions, they had

Ford's blessing and mandate to create their own unique adventure. In this way, these social media influencers could express their own interests, passions, and personalities through the way they chose to carry out the missions.

One way Ford facilitated this was to give agents the opportunity to support causes important to them. For instance, during Social Awareness Month, agent Natasha was able to draw attention to the need for such community programs as Meals on Wheels by dressing up in crazy costumes and delivering food to those in need. Agent Alison used her Fiesta to collect books for overseas troops from dozens of locations. (Then she had to figure out how she was going to ship them!)

By acknowledging and valuing the individual personalities and values of its agents—and by extension, its agents' communities—Ford was able to provide an outlet for personal expression and individuality that had nothing to do with the features of the Fiesta!

4. Ford rewarded loyal Ford customers.

An important component of the Fiesta Movement was the idea of "fair trade." Instead of simply asking this group of "culture creators" to spread the word about the Fiesta, Ford gave them something in return. I am not just talking about the use of a supercool car. They received adventure, the opportunity to expand their influence online, and experiences that allowed them to generate a steady stream of new and exciting content for their communities.

Bud Caddell, a strategist behind the campaign, said in the *Harvard Business Review Blog Network*:

> *The idea was: let's go find twenty-something YouTube storytellers who've learned how to earn a fan community of their own. [People] who can craft a true narrative inside video, and let's go talk to them. And let's put them inside situations that they don't get to normally experience/document. Let's add value back to their life. They're always looking, they're always hungry, they're always looking for more content to create. I think this gets things exactly right.*

What Is a Community?

Ford was able to leverage its agents' strong, preexisting communities and create a responsive, enthusiastic community of its own. But *what is a community*, particularly when we are talking about businesses and brands? We all know of such communities as church congregations, school PTAs, and nonprofit organizations. Many of these types of communities are, in part, regionally based; however, their underlying tenets are shared values, interests, or goals.

I opened this chapter with the definition of "community": "a feeling of fellowship with others, as a result of sharing common attitudes, interests, and goals." To help you understand more fully the concept of community in practice, I thought it would be helpful to talk about well-known, vibrant communities that are bringing like-minded people together with pretty amazing results.

Comic-Con

For those unfamiliar with it, Comic-Con is the largest gathering of comic book enthusiasts in the world. Held each year in San Diego, the convention draws up to 130,000 fans from around the world.

Attendees spend time hobnobbing with cult celebrities, buying and selling sci-fi and pop culture memorabilia, dressing up in elaborate costumes, and participating in celebrity panels and hands-on workshops. More importantly, perhaps, is the sense of community that dominates the event.

Attendees frequently speak of the important friendships they have made through the event—in many cases, friendships sustained only through their once-a-year contact at the conventions and through social media (nearly half a million people "Like" the Comic-Con Facebook Fan Page). In spite of this infrequent in-person contact, long-term, meaningful connections are formed, the foundation being a shared passion for comics and pop culture.

Matt Forbeck, in his book *The Con Job*, speaks of the almost magical sense of community that takes place at these events:

> *It struck Sophie that Comic-Con was something like a modern-day Brigadoon, a thriving city of a hundred and fifty thousand people that sprang up here in San Diego for less than a week every summer. People flocked to it from across the nation and around the world to populate it for its all-too-short existence, played their chosen roles, then dispersed back to their real homes as soon as the city disappeared. And the next summer, they'd do it all over again, forming a living history of their own in annual installments.*

Harley-Davidson

When you hear the name Harley-Davidson, what comes to mind? If I had to venture a guess, I would say motorcycles (I am clever that way). But if that is as far as your line of thought takes you, you are missing the bigger picture.

For instance, did you know you can find Harley-Davidson branded furniture, watches, baby clothes, and even *bathroom faucets*? Whatever product you are in the market for, likely a Harley-Davidson branded version exists.

A quick Google search for Harley-Davidson reveals a far more involved, intricate, and hard-core community of motorcycle enthusiasts. Fans of these powerful bikes can become official "members," joining the more than 1 million participating in online membership groups and local chapter meetings. In addition, smaller, equally enthusiastic membership groups exist to meet the needs of minority riders. The Harlistas group is for Latino riders, the Iron Elite group is for African-American riders, and a group even exists for military and veteran riders.

For these enthusiasts, owning and riding a Harley is about far more than having a really nice bike. It is about being part of a larger community of liked-minded people who understand and share a fierce passion for the riding culture.

This isn't just about a motorbike anymore; this is about a way of life.

Susan G. Komen Breast Cancer Awareness Foundation

As breast cancer victim Susan Komen moved into her final days of life, her sister promised she would do everything in her power to find a cure for the disease. Susan's sister,

Nancy G. Brinker, has certainly kept that promise. In the more than thirty years since the Susan G. Komen Breast Cancer Foundation was formed, it has raised almost $1.5 billion for cancer research.

The annual Race for the Cure is the single largest fundraising event for breast cancer, supporting innovative local and international breast cancer research and the mobilization of millions of supporters and advocates.

According to the Susan G. Komen for the Cure website, the foundation is built on a community of people making a difference. As the "boldest community fueling the best science and making the biggest impact in the fight against breast cancer," the foundation is built on the communal goal of putting an end to the disease. I don't doubt for a second that when a cure for breast cancer is found, this dedicated and passionate community will be responsible in no small part.

How Do You Connect with a Community?

In the three examples, we see strong communities of individuals who have come together because of shared passions, interests, values, or goals. Online, we find communities exist for the same reasons.

But how, as marketers, do we participate in and connect with preestablished communities? How do we join communities without being intrusive? How do we add value to these communities?

First, let's look at how ***not*** to behave in community.

The Wrong Ways to Behave in a Community

Being pushy and advertising—We all know marketers who join online communities simply to advertise their business or products. They can somehow bring every comment back to their product and use the forum to unabashedly promote their business.

Being controlling—Previously, we have talked about how smart brands know they no longer control the conversation. But this doesn't stop some marketers from giving it their best shot! Authentic marketers give input into a conversation; they don't try to control it.

Being a know-it-all—No one likes a know-it-all—including on social media. When you join an existing community online, it is important to speak with humility and be willing to honor other viewpoints you may not share or agree with. There is nothing wrong with sharing what you know, but understand you aren't the be-all and end-all of information sources!

Spamming community members—Chances are, those who have joined an online community haven't done so to receive spam, sales pitches, or private messages. In fact, this is generally a great way to get kicked out of a group, PRONTO!

The *Right* Way to Behave in a Community

In his bestselling book *Youtility*, social media guru Jay Baer emphasizes the importance of being helpful and *useful* to your community. In the book's preface, he writes: "The difference between helping and selling is just 2 letters. But those letters make all the difference. Your company needs to become a YOUtility. Sell something, and you make a customer. Help someone, and you make a customer for life."

When you join other people's communities (OPCs) for the sole purpose of selling your product or advertising your services, you may get a few quick sales in the short term, but in the long term, you certainly won't gain much trust. I would even challenge that you would get a few sales in the short term. It is only by offering true value to a community that you become an indispensable member—a trusted, valued, and integral part of the community.

You can offer value to your community in various ways that will go a long way toward building authentic relationships with those around you. Providing a new perspective through sharing useful information; offering support, feedback, and thoughtful opinions; and providing humble, servant-based leadership are all ways you can become a welcome and valued member of a community.

Finding, Joining, and Becoming a Useful Member of OPCs

Knowing how to become a valued and helpful member of a preexisting community is one thing, but many marketers struggle with figuring out *which* online communities are the most beneficial to join. With thousands of groups on Facebook alone, is it any wonder many marketers experience "analysis paralysis"?

This section will outline briefly a strategy for finding your desired demographic communities on social media, and then give practical tips for becoming a valued member of those groups.

1. Define your target demographic, and figure out where these people are hanging out.

Although this goes beyond the scope of this chapter, determining the demographic of your target market is a critical first step to finding your community online. As we have talked about, different social networks appeal to different genders, age groups, and personality types.

For instance, if your target demographic is twenty-something male "techies," finding relevant Google+ circles likely will yield positive and rewarding results. Or if your target market is largely made up of professionals or academics, you will have the best chance of finding them on LinkedIn or Twitter.

2. Search for groups.

Every major social media site provides a way to segment its population. For instance, Facebook has groups—open, closed, and secret, Google+ has circles, and YouTube has subscriptions. These groups can be formed based on demographics, location, interest, or any number of other factors.

The important thing is to figure out to which groups you will be able to add the most value and impact. In this sense, joining the biggest, "most exciting" group may not always be the best move. When deciding which groups to join, ask yourself:

- What unique knowledge or information can I contribute to the group?
- In what ways could I be a unique and valued member of this community?
- How am I different from others in this community?
- What can I bring to the table that members would appreciate?

3. Behave as a valued member, and you'll become valued.

Once you have joined a group, it is time to figure out how you can become a valued participant. While this may sound obvious, *behaving as a valued member inevitably will help you become truly valued.*

By offering useful information, thoughtful opinions, and generous support to those around you, you're behaving in a meaningful and authentic way, adding true value to the community. Practical ways you can add value to a group may include:

- Offering support and guidance when a group member is struggling.
- Asking thought-provoking questions to get a lively conversation going.
- Providing relevant and thoughtful responses to comments or questions.
- Providing gentle leadership when conflict or disagreements arise between group members.

How Does Joining a Group Help Me Sell My Product?

I'm sure some readers are thinking this already: How does joining a group help me sell my product? What is the point of being part of a community if it doesn't contribute to the bottom line?

While I hear and understand what you are saying, it is exactly this question that often leads marketers down the slippery slope from well-intentioned salesperson to full-out social media spammer.

As I have talked about often throughout this book, we have moved away from traditional "push" marketing and are firmly entrenched in the age of "pull" marketing. This means attracting customers, not pushing a message at them. It means offering true value, not hype or feigned excitement. It means participating in the conversation, not trying to control it.

All these concepts are of particular importance when you're part of OPCs. Authentic marketers know that in the Internet age, where consumers control the conversation, providing value is the one and only way to build trust and long-term, profitable relationships.

Building Your Own Community

You may be asking, "Why all this talk about joining other people's communities? Why not just start my own?" Good questions. There are definite advantages to creating and building your own community; while being part of other people's communities is a valuable way to join the conversation, building your own community comes with its own distinct benefits. They include:

The ability to control your membership—Unlike with OPCs, when you have established your own community, you have the ability to control (to some extent) who becomes a member. For instance, as an admin on a Facebook group, you have the capacity to remove members who may be disruptive or who may not be abiding by the group's rules.

Greater control over the target demographic—Because you can choose which social network you will build your community on, you also have greater control over the target demographic with which you are looking to engage. For instance, if your target market is more likely to be using Google+, you can choose to build a community there. On the other hand, OPCs may be built on platforms that are not ideal for your target market, and there is nothing you can do about it. The good news is this offers an amazing opportunity for you to create a community and fill the need for a connection point.

A capacity to guide the conversation—When you have your own community, you have an increased capacity to guide the direction of the conversation. Your voice is amplified, as people are there, in part, to hear what you (specifically ***you***) have to say. It will be your role to provide valuable content to your community, and this way you have a greater capacity to provide direction to the themes and topics that will be covered and to the perspectives that will be given.

Increased leadership and authority—Your community will be looking to you, as an administrator of a group, to give direction and guidance. As a leader, it is your role to set the tone and values of the group, so if you value honesty and transparency, for instance (which I hope you do!), you can build your community around these values. In OPCs the values may be significantly different, and you have no authority to change them.

Greater control with calls to action—With your own community, you have a greater ability to spur your members to action using strong calls to action. In OPCs, your voice is one of many, and your calls to action could be called on the carpet by that community leader. However, when you are the one providing the content, you can incorporate calls to action wherever appropriate.

When it comes down to it, having your own community, while taking significantly more work and effort, will go much further in terms of helping you meet your objectives, providing value to your audience, and helping you to be heard in the conversation.

Remember that the rules of "pull" marketing apply here and are perhaps even more important when you have the privilege of working with your own community: Be consistent, ask questions, request feedback, and provide valuable content. By doing these things consistently, you will be contributing to the growth, strength, and vibrancy of your community, all of which ultimately will lead to a stronger, healthier brand.

Final Thoughts

At the beginning of this chapter, we talked about how Ford leveraged the power of existing communities, as well as building its own community, to increase awareness of the Ford Fiesta. Ford knew the power of community to get people excited, engaged, and enthusiastically participating in a conversation about its product.

By recruiting individuals who had already built significant communities consistent with Ford's target demographic (millennials), the company was able to generate increased awareness and interest in the Fiesta at a relatively low cost, compared with traditional advertising. The fact that Ford experienced record sales of twenty-three thousand units in the second half of 2010 alone provided the proof that this risky campaign was ultimately worthwhile.

The question for you is, how can you utilize the power of community—both yours and other people's—to engage, excite, and inspire your target demographic? How can you help educate and empower your community members? How can you guide the conversation in a way that increases awareness of your brand's values and products?

EXERCISE:

Finding an online community you can participate in doesn't have to be complicated. Take a few minutes to work through the steps below to find a great product-, service-, and/or brand-focused community to join on Facebook.

1. Go to Facebook.
2. Use Graph Search and enter "Groups about ____________." Fill in the blank with your interest. For instance, if you are a coffee wholesaler, you could enter "Groups about coffee" or even search for "Groups about Starbucks." It stands to reason if people are talking about Starbucks, they like coffee, right?
3. Search for open groups, as there is no barrier to joining them.
4. Review the group's membership and feed to see if it has the type of people and is the type of group it makes sense for you to join. If so, join the group.
5. Become a "useful" member of that group, as defined previously.

CHAPTER 7

AUTHENTIC MARKETERS UNDERSTAND VIRALITY

"Spritz the bowl before you go,
and no one else will ever know."

What are we talking about in the quote above, and when you find out, will you be offended?

If you spent any time online in the winter of 2013, that quote, from an ad campaign by Poo-Pourri, will not come as a shock. Its latest and most well-known campaign, based on a single YouTube video showing an attractive female, well, indisposed, promised that if you used its bathroom spray, you would "leave the toilet smelling better than you found it."

To date, the company has experienced a *13,000 percent increase in website traffic* directly attributed to the video, and has sold more than four million units of the spray.

So what is the secret behind this campaign and many others like it? How does a single video take a company from fledgling startup to being mentioned in a book (not to mention those massive sales)?

Virality.

Virality is a word that did not exist a decade ago, but that is now something marketers everywhere dream of and lust after. It is powerful online, accelerated word-of-mouth marketing that serves as a turbo jet engine, pushing along a product or service.

Earlier we talked about how marketing has changed over the course of history. To recap, in ancient times, businesses succeeded or failed based largely on what customers were saying about them. This was word-of-mouth marketing at its most basic.

As we moved into the communication age, in which big brands dominated the conversation through massive ad campaigns and millions of "impressions," word of mouth was still alive and well, although it wasn't as easy to recognize. Marketing campaigns were focused on bombarding people with impressions in hopes that a small percentage would at least try their products. Some would, but the real success came not just when people tried the products, but *when they told somebody else about them.* It was still word-of-mouth marketing, but at an accelerated pace and a much higher cost than just allowing nature to take its course.

Now, as we have moved into the Internet age, in which geography and capital are no longer limiting factors, word of mouth has become hyper-accelerated. Whereas brands could achieve massive exposure through TV and radio ads just ten or twenty years ago, they also needed corresponding budgets to achieve the results they wanted. Now small, virtually unknown brands can become household names in a very short amount of time, for a relatively small investment. For the first time ever, small business owners can be competitive with larger, well-funded brands.

The rate at which a piece of content can spread via social media—whether it is a video, photo, or article—is astonishing. Think about it—the average Facebook user has about four hundred "friends." Each of those friends

has about four hundred friends. So, just two levels down, that is 160,000 possible connections (400 x 400). Three levels down, that is *64 million possible connections* (400 x 400 x 400). Reaching that kind of audience would have been impossible for small businesses just a few years ago. The really interesting part? It is FREE!

This concept should have marketers licking their lips.

What Does Real Virality Look Like?

Before we dive into the pros and cons of virality, it is important to note that as we talk about virality throughout this chapter, we are not just referring to the sorts of hyper-viral campaigns that launch companies into superstardom. Yes, virality certainly can look like that. But considering that most marketers will never achieve that level of virality, where does that leave the rest of us?

As you read through this chapter, keep in mind that virality simply refers to a piece of content being *circulated rapidly around the web.* This can mean a video that gets ten million views, but it can also mean a blog post that gets one thousand shares or a photo on your website that gets ten thousand views. While virality that happens on a smaller scale may not catapult a company to instant success, it certainly can help drive an increase in brand awareness, as well as in many of the metrics we, as marketers, focus on: website visitors, page views, and, ultimately, sales.

The Pros and Cons of Virality

In light of these benefits, it may seem like virality is the "golden ticket" for marketers in the digital age. But, as with anything in life, it comes with its own unique set of challenges. Before you decide to jump in headfirst and pursue a viral marketing strategy for your business, let's briefly discuss the pros and cons of virality for your business.

Pros of Viral Marketing

It Can Result in Massive Exposure

Having a video, blog post, or photo go viral is, hands down, the most cost-effective way to gain massive exposure for your product or business. A single piece of viral content has the potential to drive huge amounts of traffic, media attention, and buzz to a product or brand. Through the power of social media, it can be shared hundreds of thousands or even millions of times in a mind-bogglingly short amount of time.

It's Relatively Inexpensive

Compared with traditional methods of advertising, such as TV or radio ads, and even compared with some forms of social media marketing, having your content go viral is far more cost-effective. Most costs are related to the creation or production of your content, although for more elaborate campaigns, other, more substantial costs can be incurred (more on this later).

It Has an Overflow Effect

One of the effects of your content going viral is that it can result in increased exposure for your website and other types of content. People who have enjoyed your photo, video, or blog post are more likely to want to find out more about your business and your other products. This can lead to increased visitors, impressions, and page views.

Cons of Viral Marketing

The downside to virality isn't something that gets talked about a lot. I think many marketers hold virality as the pinnacle of online marketing: a cost-effective way to reach a huge audience in a short amount of time. However, virality isn't without its problems. Here are a few:

Virality Is Difficult to Create and Predict

Unlike with some other methods of marketing, there is no "formula" or precise framework you can follow to make your content go viral. In fact, in some cases, the very act of *trying* to make something go viral can have just the opposite effect.

Since viral content often tends toward the quirky, shocking, and unexpected, there is always the potential for it to generate a significant amount of *negative* buzz for your brand.

Virality Is Hard to Follow Up

The majority of viral content that exists is of, as we say, "one-hit wonders." For reasons often unknown, a particular piece of content goes viral, and any attempts to build on the success of that virality fail. Just because you have done it once doesn't mean you can do it again.

Virality Can Have Unintended Backlash

While a successful campaign can generate massive amounts of exposure for your product or brand, it also has the potential to generate massive amounts of negative sentiment.

Event the best-laid plans can go awry. Content meant to be shockingly funny potentially can be seen as shockingly offensive. This can result in backlash from certain groups or demographics, taking your campaign in a very different direction from what you had intended.

Virality Is Difficult to Translate into Sales

Having your content go viral is no guarantee that you will experience a corresponding increase in sales. Because viral content typically doesn't include the standard ad copy element of a call to action, what the viewers do with what they have seen is out of your hands.

Creating Virality

As I discussed this chapter with colleagues, we joked about including an exercise on "how to create your own viral content." I won't go into the details, but let's just say it involved a video camera, your dog, a clown costume, and a pool.

In all seriousness, there is no surefire formula for creating virality. That said, some channels will help you scale your campaign to give it the best chance of going viral. For your content—whether a piece of information, a video, or an image—to get in front of an audience, you will need to decide which channels you are going to use to get it there.

Virality Is Born from Appealing Content

Producing great content that has a chance of going viral can be done either in-house or by a third party. In fact, a whole industry has emerged specifically to help businesses create and promote viral content. Some Google ads I've seen recently include:

> "Word of Mouth Campaigns: Target Consumers, Ignite Discussion."

"Make a Video Go Viral: Millions of Views for Your Video."

And my favorite:

"I will create a viral Facebook contest on your fan page for $5."

If only it were that simple! As I mentioned, virality is difficult to create or predict. I love Seth Godin's views on virality. When asked how to write copy that goes viral, Seth's response is:

The best approach is to write for just one person. Make an impact on just one person. Even better, make it so they can't sleep that night unless they choose to make a difference for just one other person

by sharing your message with them. The rest will take care of itself.

Old Spice has done a terrific job of creating viral content. In fact, the company is one of the few that have managed to recreate a "virality recipe," so to speak. The video, featuring an attractive, scantily clad man holding a bottle of Old Spice body wash, states that you could be "with the man your man could smell like" if only he used Old Spice.

With more than 47 million views as of this writing, this video is perhaps the most viewed branded video ever created, and considering subsequent Old Spice videos have gained five, ten, and even twenty million views, it is easy to see why the company has continued using this strategy.

Ways to Increase the Likelihood of Virality

As mentioned, there is no tried-and-true formula for creating virality, but there are definitely ways you can improve your odds. They include:

Advertising

One way marketers can set the stage for a viral campaign is by investing in paid advertising. Such mediums as banner, pay-per-click, or social media ads can lay the groundwork for content to get in front of a large initial audience.

If you are relying on paid advertising to make your content go viral, however, you are going to be waiting a really long time! While paid advertising certainly can get the ball rolling in terms of gaining page views or impressions, the content ultimately will have to be engaging and exciting enough of its own accord to truly go viral. Its viewers still will need to have the will and desire to share the content; no amount of advertising can force this type of word-of-mouth marketing.

Using Online Influencers

In an attempt to achieve virality, some marketers find, buy, or build a community of online influencers who can help promote their content and potentially help it go viral. Every niche has them: groups of influential social media leaders and bloggers who have built loyal, established communities on Facebook and Twitter.

By enlisting the help of these influencers, businesses and brands can reach large numbers of people by leveraging their popularity and influence.

Enlisting the Help of Employees

Another method businesses sometimes use to help achieve virality is enlisting the help of their employees. For instance, by asking employees to use their personal social media accounts to help spread a piece of content, businesses may achieve greater reach than they could on their own.

Businesses may ask their employees to help in this manner, offer incentives for doing so, or even at times *require* their employees to help (please note: I am not suggesting you do this!). I will say this: If you have built a great culture in your company, your employees will *want* to share and spread the word about whatever your company is involved with at any given time.

Building a Massive Community to Serve as a Launching Platform

One of the most effective ways to jump-start a viral campaign is by promoting it to your community. However, for this to work, your community generally has to be a pretty good size. This makes it a strategy that will take great patience, perseverance, and a whole lot of hard work! Building a massive online community takes time, but in the end, it is also perhaps the most authentic channel for jump-starting viral content.

People often ask me how I have managed to build a massive community on social media: 55,000 Facebook fans, 210,000 Twitter followers, 25,000 LinkedIn connections, and 50,000 email subscribers. Fortunately, I have an easy answer: by following the principles of authentic marketing as laid out in this book.

When you already have a massive community, jump-starting a viral campaign gets a whole lot easier; you already know the pain points, values, and preferred modes of communication of your members, and you already have given them reason to trust you.

Common Elements of Viral Content

Although virality is unpredictable and hard to recreate, research is being done on what human elements are common within viral content. Professor Jonah Berger of the University of Pennsylvania is doing some fascinating research into factors that make ideas and products go viral. He and his colleagues set out to analyze which *New York Times* articles went viral in terms of being shared via email.

Although we have to be careful to consider the fact that this study was done on news-based content, as opposed to humorous, educational, or commercial content, the results also could be useful for digital marketers from other niches.

Berger and his colleagues found that the content that had the greatest likelihood of going viral was:

- **Surprising**—It included a sense of the unexpected, like chickens roaming the streets of New York.
- **Intense**—More emotional stories were more likely to be shared.
- **Positive**—People preferred articles with positive themes, ones that made them *feel good.*
- **Longer**—Surprisingly, longer, more intellectually challenging articles were more likely to get shared.

- **Awe-inspiring**—Stories that made a reader broaden his or her views and experience a sense of something greater than self were among the most shared.

When creating your own content, it certainly doesn't hurt to incorporate some of these elements and see what happens.

Translating Virality into Sales

Now it is time for the ten-million-dollar question: If you do manage to have something go viral, how does this translate into sales? What ways do marketers capitalize on their viral content to increase the bottom line?

As I see it, there are two main ways:

Directly

I'll start by saying this is *not* a method I recommend. While a rare few marketers have used this method with success, more often than not, it results in alienating viewers, rather than attracting them to your products or business.

One way you can directly market to your audience is by incorporating a call to action within your content. For instance, if you produce a video, you could include a line at the end like, "Click the button below to order now." Although we're so used to using strong calls to action in our marketing copy, this is one area where marketers need to tread carefully. Generally speaking, successful viral content does *not* include a call to action.

Another way you can directly market within your viral content is by making an offer. This could be a coupon code, a discount, or even a trial product. Generally speaking, however, even this is something I would avoid.

Indirectly

We have talked a lot about how, in the Internet age, consumers control the conversation. Part of capitalizing on virality is letting go of the control you think you should have over your viewers and customers. When you think of viral content as a way to directly sell, you are missing the point. Viral content is more about creating an image for your brand and helping people associate your brand with fun, excitement, or awe (or whatever feeling your viral content evokes).

That said, there are ways virality ultimately can lead to increased sales:

- People may come to associate your brand or products with being "fun," "cool," or "exciting" because of your campaign. This can lead to increased interest in your brand and, ultimately, to increased sales.
- By creating and promoting multiple pieces of content, you potentially can hold the attention of viewers for a longer period of time. For

instance, by creating multiple YouTube videos and setting them to play one after the other, you can potentially increase impressions.

- Perhaps the best way to leverage the success of your viral content is by moving people to other places where you *can* convert them. For instance, if you can find a way to entice viewers to your website, you could directly convert them or get them into your online sales funnel.

Virality in Action: The Dollar Shave Club

At the beginning of this chapter, we talked about Poo-Pourri, a small business that was able to take a common, everyday activity and, using humor, turn it into something people *wanted* to share. I mean, let's face it: There are more glamorous products out there than bathroom spray. Yet even with this obvious challenge, the company was able to achieve amazing results.

Another company that has managed to gain massive exposure and revenue, in spite of having a less-than-sexy product, is the Dollar Shave Club. The idea behind the company is this: Rather than paying for expensive razor blade replacements month after month, the club will mail you high-quality razors for only a few dollars per month.

It is easy to see why the ninety-second video, which features co-founder Michael Dubin walking around the company warehouse, claiming the company's blades are "f***ing great," has gotten the reach it has: It's irreverently funny and unexpected, and successfully manages to walk the line between being crass and a bit self-deprecating.

The video, created by a professional production crew, had amazing results. The company gained twelve thousand new customers in the first two days after the video was released, and to date has garnered more than twelve million views on YouTube—and all this for an investment of only forty-five hundred dollars for video production. (It should be noted that the video was done as a personal favor to Michael Dubin at a seriously discounted rate; a video of this quality typically would run about fifty thousand dollars.) That said, there are many instances where amateur or "on the fly" videos have gone viral and created great visibility for brands.

In any case, for a relatively small financial investment, the video has managed to single-handedly build the company. So how did the company do it? What elements of this campaign can we implement in our own viral marketing strategies?

The Company Used Humor

There is no question that using humor can help you connect with your audience. It has the unique ability to make your product or business seem more relatable, personable, and down-to-earth. It allows you to poke fun at life's challenges and events in a way that makes people say, "Yes! That's so true!"

Michael Dubin and his team clearly understood how to harness the power of humor to connect with their audience. Unlike with traditional advertising, viewers of the video *chose* to watch it; watching wasn't required. Although the goal of the video—to gain new customers for the club—was obvious, the video was humorous enough that viewers didn't feel as if they were being "sold to." They were being entertained, first and foremost.

Featuring a toddler shaving her dad's head, a huge stuffed bear (that bear is still a bit of a mystery to me), and Dubin and Alejandra (a warehouse employee) taking a ride through the warehouse in a children's wagon, it's just random and absurd enough to avoid being cliché.

The Company Was Authentic

As noted, the goal of the video was obvious: to get people to sign up for the monthly razor delivery service. The video was related to the product, and the marketing message was clear and transparent: You should want to buy our razors because they are good quality, and it will save you a ton of money.

Of course, it didn't hurt that the underlying values of the company also were based on authenticity. Rather than trying to compete with the big guys, such as Bic and Gillette, by selling dirt-cheap razors and then making huge profits on subsequent blade sales, the company chose an authentic business model: selling basic, good-quality razors at a great price.

The Company Relied Entirely on Social Media

With the exception of some Google PPC ads at the outset of the campaign, the company relied entirely on social media shares to take its video viral. These views were not the result of banner advertising, carefully planned SEO efforts, or even social media advertising. The video gained its twelve million views *because people liked it and wanted to share it on social media.*

Through a single video, the Dollar Shave Club has been able to level the playing field, competing with huge, multinational corporations. For a relatively small investment, the company has managed not only to achieve massive exposure for its brand, but also to translate this into sales.

It is important to note that the company did it all *while being authentic.*

Chapter 8

WHAT HAPPENS WHEN AUTHENTICITY BACKFIRES?

"In this ever-changing society, the most powerful and enduring brands are built from the heart. They are real and sustainable. Their foundations are stronger because they are built with the strength of the human spirit, not an ad campaign. The companies that are lasting are those that are authentic."
—**Howard Schultz**, Pour Your Heart Into It: How Starbucks Built a Company One Cup at a Time

Throughout this book, we have talked about authenticity and how businesses that are built on such principles as honesty and transparency are setting themselves apart and building long-term, profitable relationships. In a climate where many business owners are still stuck on traditional "push" methods of marketing, marketers who are able to authentically connect with their target market have a clear advantage.

We know consumers relate better to people and companies that are "being themselves"—no fronts, no pretenses, no hidden motives. Companies that are able to be transparent and share how they feel about things and how they look at the world are more likely to gain the trust and respect of current and potential customers, ultimately leading to stronger, further-reaching, and more monetizable relationships.

However, authenticity can be a double-edged sword. While marketers should strive for it, openness and transparency *can* have unintended consequences. For instance, by openly expressing an opinion on something, you could face criticism from those who don't share your opinion. Also, since words can mean different things to different people, or can be misconstrued, it is possible to offend entire races, nationalities, groups, or interests without intending to do so. Finally, and sadly, there are legions of faceless, nameless "trolls" who subversively scour the Internet, looking for places to create a problem.

So what happens when, despite your best efforts, something *does* goes wrong? What do you do when authenticity backfires, and you are left picking up the pieces of your damaged reputation and trying to repair damaged relationships?

Authenticity Backfiring

One way we can begin to figure out strategies for dealing with, and hopefully avoiding, these kinds of situations is by looking at how other companies have responded when faced with this challenge. In the three examples I will discuss, you will see exactly how damaging a breakdown in authenticity can be.

HMV Employee Tweets Mass Firing Live

When music retailer HMV decided to fire almost two hundred of its employees, little did it know that the entire grisly situation was being tweeted live by a member of the company's social media team. The tweets to HMV's sixty-five thousand followers included:

"We are live tweeting from HR, where we are all being fired!"

"Sorry we've been quiet for so long. Under contract we've been unable to say a word—or more importantly—tell the truth."

Can't you just imagine the chaos that ensued when management got wind of the situation? Using the hashtag #hmvXFactorFiring, word had spread with

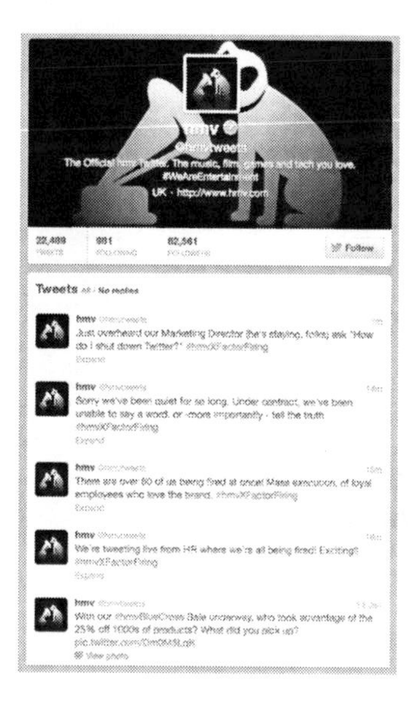

lightning speed throughout the Twitter-sphere and across the web. Although management was quick to delete the offending tweets, as we know, nothing on the web is ever truly *gone.* News of the debacle continued to spread on social media long after the original tweets disappeared.

Rather than addressing the negative tweets head-on, the company chose to delete the tweets and try to sweep them under the rug. This tweet from the above-mentioned employee pretty much summarizes the company's response:

"Just overheard our Marketing Director (he's staying, folks) ask, "How do I shut down Twitter?"

Not cool!

Luton Airport Uses Fatal Crash
Picture in Facebook Update

A member of the social media team for London Luton Airport posted a picture of a plane crash with the caption, "Because we are such a super airport . . . this is what we prevent you from when it snows. . . . Weeeee." While the employee who posted this probably had no idea, it turned out that a six-year-old child had been killed in the crash depicted in the photo.

Facebook fans were quick to point out the company's error:

"I am pretty appalled that this is your official page and that this is the image and wording you use."

"Poor form really, as a child died in this incident."

"This is so inappropriate and should be removed immediately; it is certainly not something that should be taken so lightly and made fun of."

To its credit, the company was quick to remove the offending post and respond with a full-out apology. The company referred to the staff member as "new" and "overenthusiastic," but also took responsibility for the insensitivity of the post.

This is a situation in which, despite allegedly having social media guidelines in place, a grievous error occurred. This is a good reminder to businesses that mistakes can happen—*even* when you have a social media plan in place. Fortunately, it appears the airport's plan also laid out the appropriate course of action to pursue if and when a situation arose, and Luton's response likely went a long way toward restoring faith in the organization.

J.P. Morgan's Disastrous Twitter Q&A Session

On the very day that J.P. Morgan underwrote Twitter's initial public offering, J.P. Morgan decided to hold a Twitter Q&A, where young finance hopefuls could converse with the company using the hashtag #AskJPM. The question of the day? "What career advice would you ask a leading exec at a global firm?"

Great question, right? It would initiate dialogue between company executives and eager econ students. What J.P. Morgan failed to take into account, however, was how the company's recent and well-publicized legal problems would affect the chat, not to mention, one of the execs moderating the chat was Jimmy Lee, who, according to the J.P. Morgan website, "has financed and advised on many of the most historic transactions in the United States."

While the company was hoping for innocuous questions like, "What university courses should I take to prepare myself for a finance career?" they instead received questions like:

"Did you always want to be part of a vast, corrupt, criminal enterprise, or did you 'break bad'?"

"Did you have a specific number of people's lives you needed to ruin before you considered your business model a success?"

"What section of the poor and disenfranchised have you yet to exploit for profit, and how are you working to address that?"

Needless to say, the company quickly saw the error of its ways. After the first day of questioning, it sent out a tweet: "Tomorrow's Q&A is canceled. Bad idea. Back to the drawing board."

Sometimes "good ideas" can quickly spiral out of control. If that happens, own that it was a bad idea, apologize when and where necessary, and move on.

Common Traits of Epic Fails

It is easy in hindsight to identify what went wrong in each of those "fails." But you know what they say:

Hindsight is twenty-twenty. In "real life," it can be more difficult to identify and predict situations or actions that can lead to such unintended and harmful consequences.

In this section of the chapter, we will look at some common characteristics of authenticity meltdowns. It is only by identifying what went wrong that we can hope to discover what traps we ourselves can avoid!

A Company Does Something Stupid or Insensitive

This much is clear: In each of the previous examples, the trigger for the fail was the business (or a representative of the business) *doing something stupid.* Common sense went out the window, and actions were taken that the businesses wished they could take back. The actions, including poking fun at a situation in which a child died, and deciding to hold a live chat during a time when the company was vulnerable and likely to be criticized, set them up for a massive fail.

A Company Turns a Small Problem into a Big One with an Inappropriate Response

In many cases, a quick, genuine response to an error in judgment may be all that is needed to quell negative responses and salvage a company's reputation. The problem is, too many companies resist apologizing or setting things right, and instead react slowly, generically, or inappropriately.

Take Kmart, for example. The company recently took some flak for announcing it would keep its stores open Thanksgiving Day. Twitter followers responded en masse, complaining of the impact this would have on employees and their families. Kmart's response? The company armed its social media team with one hundred canned, generic responses, such as, "Kmart is staffing w/ teams and seasonal associates who when possible, giving them opportunity to make extra money during the holiday."

Probably not the best way to help your followers feel "heard," Kmart!

A Company Does Not Respond Quickly

When you offend someone face to face, you generally have a fairly large window of opportunity to make things right. But when you offend someone on social media, the effect and impact can be far more explosive. One ill-conceived comment or misinterpreted statement can be enough to quickly earn you reams of negative sentiment. Businesses have the potential to offend not just a few people, but entire races, nationalities, or groups in one fell swoop. With the hyper-accelerated nature of social media, word of a business's mistake can spread in minutes.

A Company Leaves the Power of Social Media in the Wrong Hands

There seems to be a belief in some circles that social media management is a job reserved for interns or entry-level employees. As is evidenced in the Luton Airport example, this can have disastrous results. As social media is the *face* of your company online—and, in fact, often the primary way your customers choose to connect with your company—leaving it in the hands of unqualified employees isn't something I recommend. At a minimum, you should have a seasoned, senior employee supervising and a defined set of protocols for "what happens when . . ." scenarios.

What to Do When Authenticity Backfires

Knowing some of the reasons for authenticity meltdowns is helpful, but what practical steps can you take to avoid such situations, and what do you do when all your best efforts fail? How do you respond in a way that restores trust and rebuilds relationships?

I suggest four primary ways you can reduce the likelihood of a social media meltdown:

Closely Control Who Uses Social Media in an Official Capacity

As we see in the HMV and Luton Airport examples, the responsibility for social media efforts was left in the hands of unqualified and/or disgruntled employees. Add to that the fact that apparently these employees were left largely unsupervised, without sufficient checks and balances in place, and these companies set themselves up for the perfect social media storm.

When deciding who will manage your social media efforts, keep in mind that this person will be on the front lines of the conversations with your community. Rather than choosing someone simply because he or she is "young" and has good social media or technical skills, ask yourself, *Who do we want to represent our brand online? Who do we want to be the voice of our brand? Does this person have the maturity to respond in a manner consistent with our values?*

Think Before You Hit "Send"

This seems like common sense, but I wonder how many social media disasters could have been avoided if the person posting had simply taken a second to really think before posting. Before you hit "send," ask yourself, *Is what I am saying clear and concise? Is what I wrote what I meant to write? Was I angry, frustrated, sad, or unhappy when I wrote it? Could anything I wrote be misconstrued as offensive or hurtful?*

If you have any reservations about what you are about to post, leave the post on the back burner for an hour or two, and then come back to it with fresh eyes. You may find the post is just fine, or you may decide it is too risky and not worth it. Either way, at least you will be sure.

Get a Second Set of Eyes Involved

Smart marketers know they aren't perfect, so they surround themselves with teams and people they trust. If you are at all worried about a post or campaign offending somebody, ask for a second opinion, or don't send it. While it is possible for two (or more) people to make an error in judgment, it is far less likely.

Ask a team member or colleague, "Could this be misinterpreted? Is the wording clear, and does it convey what I am trying to say? Is this worth the risk of posting, or is it better to leave it?"

Test the Campaign Ahead of Time

If you have concerns about a potential campaign, run a focus group, and take your campaign for a trial run. This will be easier for bigger companies that have larger budgets; however, even small companies can run focus groups via email or online message boards. A potential problem can emerge when running focus groups on social media, so I wouldn't recommend testing out risqué or potentially offensive campaigns in this way. A trial run on social media can quickly turn into the "real thing" as people share your campaign with their friends.

How to Minimize the Impact of an Authenticity Meltdown

Despite your best efforts, you or someone in your organization may still slip up and say or do something unfortunate on social media. What do you do when this happens? What steps can you take to fix your mistake, rebuild relationships, and restore your reputation?

Respond Quickly

Speed is critical. Every moment you don't respond leaves the door open for your mistake to go viral. This is why a social media contingency plan is so important. In the heat of the moment, it can be difficult to know what steps need to be taken.

For instance, imagine you hear about a company that, possibly inadvertently, has offended an entire ethnicity of people. You visit the group's Facebook page to see what all the hubbub is about. Now, imagine you see the offending post, but also see the company has responded with an explanation and a sincere apology. Many times the "fail" will stop right here. You are far less likely to share the situation with others, as it has been resolved, and the drama that can ensue from such posts has petered out.

Respond Authentically

Part of responding authentically means accepting responsibility and doing your best to make it right. Most of us teach our kids to take responsibility for their actions, so why is it such a difficult concept for some marketers and business owners?

Taking time to look at the situation from another's point of view can be extremely helpful and can give you deeper insight into the feelings of those who have been hurt. A simple, sincere apology and an acknowledgment that "we screwed up" can go a long way toward defusing the situation and restoring trust. People don't mind nearly as much when you "screw up" if you fix the problem.

The Last Resort: Pull the Post

If a critical, unfixable mistake has been made, it may be appropriate to simply pull the post. This *doesn't* mean avoiding responsibility for the mistake or pretending it never happened. It *does* mean retracting an insensitive or offensive post so as to not hurt anyone else.

It is important to be transparent about the situation. However, it also can be necessary to stop the situation from getting even uglier and more out of control. Before you delete it, remember to copy it all for future reference—if only as a reminder of *what never to do again*!

Is Authenticity Worth It?

As we have seen throughout this book, the rewards of authenticity in social media are dramatic, but being authentic also involves risks. When you choose to let the *real you stand up in social media,* you open yourself up to criticism, misinterpretation, and other unintended negative consequences.

While the risks cannot be eliminated, the likelihood of something going wrong, as well as the long-term impact, can be greatly reduced with a little forethought and planning. By implementing strategies that will decrease the likelihood of a problem occurring, and then planning exactly how you minimize the impact of any situations that do arise, you can ensure that you're prepared for any eventuality.

Although this may seem like a lot of work, as far as I am concerned, it is totally worth it. *Authenticity is worth it.* In the words of Mother Teresa, "Honesty and transparency make you vulnerable. Be honest and transparent anyway."

No one ever said authenticity was easy, but in the end, it is the only real choice for smart marketers.

EXERCISE: DEVELOP A CRISIS MANAGEMENT PLAN

1. **Establish a social media listening plan.** Catching and then reacting to a problem early is critical to minimizing its impact. To do this, you must be "listening" to what is being said about your company. What procedures do you have in place to monitor the major social media sites?
2. **Establish a "chain of command."** Who gets notified when, and how? If you are a larger company and there is a serious problem that can

jeopardize the health of the entire company, it may be appropriate to notify the CEO. Smaller issues can be handled at lower levels. It is, however, important to decide who gets told what *before* the crisis occurs.

3. **Establish a response procedure.** Every situation is different, so it is difficult to recommend any particular course of action, but general procedures typically include acknowledging the issue on the same social media site where it was initiated; apologizing, if appropriate; establishing a remedy, if necessary; and removing the post, if unmanageable.

CHAPTER 9

AUTHENTIC BRANDS THRIVE

"A product can be quickly outdated,
but a successful brand is timeless."
—Stephen King

Bigger isn't always better, at least on social media.

This is a mantra I want you to repeat in your head as you read this chapter.

While I will be focusing on five mega-brands that are "getting it right" when it comes to social media, the objective of this chapter will be to see what we can learn from how these brands connect and engage with their communities online. Yes, these brands boast numbers you or I may never reach, but size isn't *nearly* as important as being present, consistent, and authentic on social media over the long haul. Even small brands, with small numbers, can apply the principles of authenticity for amazing results. As Electronic Arts director of communities Simon Stokes. "It's not just about numbers, but about the depth and consistency of engagement."

So let's dive in. Let's take a look at five brands dominating social media both quantitatively *and* qualitatively. Then, at the end of this chapter, we will look closer at what these mega-brands have in common in terms of how they use social media to engage and connect with their communities. By taking a look at the underpinnings of each of these successes, we can deduce greater truths for our own social media strategies.

Five Brands Dominating Social Media

Starbucks: Building a Brand Through Passion

Starbucks is often mentioned as a leading example of brands "doing it right" on social media. Obviously, with

numbers like 35 million Facebook fans, 5.4 million Twitter followers, and 1.8 million followers on Instagram, the company has figured out a winning strategy—both offline and online.

Despite these mind-bogglingly high numbers, Starbucks' content is often curiously lacking in direct references to its stores or coffee. While the company does post beautiful, mouthwatering product shots, you are just as likely to see pictures of a gorgeous sunrise, a tasty food recipe, or a stunning flower arrangement. While these may seem like random and strange choices for photos, Starbucks has done an astounding job of using these images to create an *emotional connection* to its brand.

Of course, you also see offers and promotions, which, I might add, are usually met with huge fanfare. Promotions like "Stocked with joy! @StarbucksStore Christmas Blend Coffees are 25% off until 12/8," or the offer of half price Frappuccino drinks from 3 to 5 p.m. are, of course, hard to resist!

The brand, however, does far more than simply promote its products. The company has managed to keep its social strategy in line with its overall business strategy in a way that many brands have not yet managed to figure out. One of the founding principles on which Starbucks is built is authenticity, and this is evident in the way the company does social media. Founder and CEO Howard Schultz says:

> *There is a word that comes to my mind when I think about our company and our people. That word is "love." I love Starbucks because everything we've tried to do is steeped in humanity.*
>
> *Respect and dignity.*
>
> *Passion and laughter.*
>
> *Compassion, community, and responsibility.*
>
> *Authenticity.*
>
> *These are Starbucks' touchstones, the source of our pride.*

These values are readily apparent not only in Starbucks' overall business model, but also in the way the company does social media. Its posts, almost exclusively consisting of photos and images, exude passion . . .

- **Passion for coffee**—displaying gorgeous product shots of its various offerings.
- **Passion for its community**—sharing customer photos, comments, and posts. This is also evidenced in its many community-building campaigns, such as #sharejoy, a campaign meant to "help create wonder and share joy by spreading Starbucks holiday cheer with friends and family on social media."
- **Passion for responsibility**—featuring pictures of the fair-trade farmers who grow Starbucks' beans.

Starbucks is also a great example of a brand that is, in a sense, going against the best practices of social media for business. If you take a quick look at its Facebook page and Twitter feed, it quickly becomes apparent that the company rarely replies to or comments on fan posts or feedback. With the staggering numbers of fans and followers it has, this isn't surprising, especially considering that at last count, the company's social media team consisted of only five employees. In spite of this lack of dialogue, fans and brand advocates are passionate about their Starbucks coffee and about promoting and connecting with the brand.

American Airlines: Excelling at Social Customer Service

American Airlines, while having a very different social strategy than Starbucks, is excelling at using social platforms to establish trust and build relationships with its customers. Its social content, particularly on Facebook, is, above all, *helpful and personal.* With 1.1 million Facebook fans, 670,000-plus Twitter followers, and 1.7 million Google+ followers, excelling at social customer service is no small accomplishment.

Jonathan Pierce, the company's director of social media communications, on cnbc.com, says, "Our team is empowered by relating to customers, finding connections and being authentic in every response. We make sure there's a face and voice behind each post. We have a team in place that understands the trials and tribulations of travel and genuinely wants it to be a positive experience for our customers."

A quick look at the company's Facebook page reveals a brand that is highly committed to customer service. With nearly every single comment or complaint receiving a response, often within minutes, its customers take advantage of social channels, even for real-time support.

So what is the secret to American Airlines' lightning-fast responses? According to Pierce, it is due to the fact that its social media team is comprised of people from both reservations and customer relations. Rather than having an isolated team of employees who must direct difficult queries to the correct department, someone on the team generally has the knowledge and ability to respond to most questions and complaints. Of the company's social media team, he says, "This skills base in our team makes sure that customers can ask us anything on social media, from an operation to a product question."

Another key observation about American Airlines' social strategy is that the company clearly doesn't attempt to control the conversation, although it does carefully monitor and contribute to it. American Airlines obviously has a strong interest in building long-term relationships with its customers, and gives its community opportunities to, as Jonathan Pierce puts it, have "our customers tell our story."

The unique strategies American Airlines has used to help tell its story include:

- Doing a YouTube series called "Behind the Scenes at American Air," answering FAQs and giving behind-the-scenes insight into the company.
- Hosting local meet-ups to connect and form relationships with brand advocates.
- Executing a Twitter campaign, requesting customers, "Tell us where you want to go, and we'll tweet you back with great #travel ideas!"

Openly sharing its brand's story, giving customers opportunities to contribute to the story, and being a highly responsive and helpful brand are all keys to American Airlines' ongoing social media success.

Coca-Cola: Evoking Happiness

With the core concept behind Coke's marketing strategy being that people use a product because it has meaning, it would seem that helping consumers find meaning in a fizzy, sugary drink would be no easy task. However, by taking the abstract concept of meaning and defining it as *communal happiness*, the company has been able to grow massive amounts of positive sentiment for its brand.

With a clear focus on its fans—not on itself—across its social media channels, Coca-Cola has been able to build an enormous community of Coke lovers who want to take part in the brand's story. Taking a somewhat rare approach of featuring user-generated content front and center on its Facebook page, some may say Coke is taking a big risk. But with its Facebook page being "a collection of your stories showing how people from around the world have helped make Coke into what it is today," the strategy is humanistic, connects directly with the company's audience, and showcases that Coke cares! If only we could bottle that success.

Part of the beauty of Coke's story is how the page came to exist. Back in the "olden days" of Facebook, anyone could start a fan page for a brand—even a mega-brand like Coca-Cola—and that is exactly what ended up happening. Started by two uber-fans, the first Coca-Cola page wasn't even under the control or direction of the company. However, when Facebook implemented a policy that only brands themselves could manage official brand fan pages, Coke was left with a decision: take over the page, or shut it down. Its decision: take ownership of the page, but allow its two superfans to continue helping build the page, and their story. I have to say, I think this was a brilliant move on Coke's part.

Another way Coke is "getting it right" is by ensuring all its employees are well-versed in social media do's and don'ts. With comprehensive social media training for all employees, the basics of engaging via social media are covered company-wide. The training programs cover the basics of what to do (and what *not* to do) on social media, as well as how to go about being a brand advocate. For employees who are involved with social media directly, advanced training is provided. This training involves regular meetings and "high-touch training," aimed at reducing the risk of social media meltdowns.

All these strategies can be found in some form in the company's social media principles. The principles, which govern how the company will use social media, are public on its "Coca-Cola Journey" website. The company commitment, both online and offline, is to be transparent in every social media engagement, to monitor its behavior on social media, and to establish protocols for how it does social media.

Finally, by using its social media influence to draw attention to bigger issues and causes, Coke is able to capture the hearts of many of its fans—literally. The #ShowYourHeart campaign encouraged Diet Coke fans to share heart-related photos in support of American Heart Month. For every photo shared using the hashtag, Diet Coke would donate one dollar to support women's heart health programs. The campaign, which engaged followers on both Twitter and Instagram, ended up being highly successful, both as a way of raising money for a good cause and as a way to align the Coca-Cola brand with the concepts of helping and giving.

Red Bull: Associating Its Product with Adventure

Some say Red Bull has essentially built its brand using social media. Looking at the success of its social campaigns over the past few years, it is hard to disagree.

Active on all the major social networks, but particularly on Facebook, Twitter, and YouTube, it is clear that the folks at Red Bull have a clear understanding of their target market (primarily young males), as well as what type of content they want to see. With Facebook posts and tweets overwhelmingly consisting of images and videos of extreme sports and athletes, and the Twitter feeds of extreme athletes fed through to Red Bull's Facebook page, it is doing a pretty darn good job of giving its community what it wants.

Clearly, Red Bull's social media identity is more about promoting a *lifestyle*, rather than a product. It is all about adventure, rather than an energy drink. The company has managed to heavily associate itself with being cool, daring, and fun. Its posts are overwhelmingly focused on *creating a sense of adventure*, ***never*** about directly selling its product. In fact, you would be hard-pressed to find more than the occasional mention of the product.

Interestingly, contrary to what you would expect, it appears Red Bull doesn't respond to comments on Facebook. While you will find the company responding more frequently to mentions on Twitter, these make up only a very small percentage of total engagement.

So, how can this be? How can a brand achieve huge amounts of success on social media, and rarely respond to comments and queries? Isn't this one of the key social media principles authentic marketers are supposed to follow?

Yes and no.

I would never attempt this strategy unless you are sure this is what your community wants! In Red Bull's case, I think this seeming lack of engagement is a direct result of knowing its audience. It sees its role in social media as creating a sense of adventure and risk and sharing it with its community. In this way, the community comes to associate the brand with these same characteristics. For some reason, the community gladly tolerates the lack of interaction.

Perhaps it is, in part, because fans know the brand is busy working on impressive campaigns, such as the Stratos Space Jump. The campaign featured Felix Baumgartner freefalling a record twenty-four miles to earth. Think about

the marketing genius behind this campaign—associating the brand with the first human being to break the sound barrier! Viewers could watch the event live on TV or via webcast. The YouTube video alone has racked up more than thirty-five million views to date. When watching the video, it is hard not to feel a sense of being part of something bigger: breaking records, doing what has never been done.

Red Bull has managed to associate an *energy drink* with free falling from space. How cool is that? This is an association that could never be stated explicitly, no matter how great the marketing message. The results of the campaign are no less astounding. The photo the company posted to Facebook immediately after Felix's landing received 21,000 comments, 51,000 shares, and 489,000 likes. That works out to a post-engagement rate of ***19,357 percent***, as reported by Socialbakers.

Disney: Building a Community on Social Media

Operating on social media under the name "Disney Living," Disney has built one of the biggest, most loyal, and engaged fan bases existing on social media today. While Disney has a presence on all the major networks, the majority of its engagement happens on Facebook, Twitter, and YouTube. With individual accounts and pages for each of its various movies and even characters, the company manages almost three hundred pages on Facebook alone.

According to Amanda Grant, director of distribution for Disney Interactive, its social media strategy is based on building community, not on selling: "Simply put, our engagement on the platforms is centered on two main principles: reach families and Disney enthusiasts, and share content that our guests are compelled to talk about and share." A brand after my own heart!

One of the key ways Disney reaches these families is by helping to draw emotional connections between the brand and its community. Sometimes the company does this by sparking connections between the past and present: sharing photos of classic Disney characters, movies, and even of Walt Disney himself. Other times, this connection is forged by the community itself through user-generated content and conversations.

Take the Disney Baby Facebook page, for instance. Content on the Disney Baby page consists largely of discussions among community members, mostly moms. Looking at its posts, you are likely to see photos of kids wearing Disney-branded clothing, questions about where to buy Disney products, or photo albums of "baby's first Disney adventure." It should be noted as well that the social media team at Disney Baby is diligent about responding to any and all contributions—questions, photos, comments, and complaints (although, to be honest, you would be hard-pressed to find more than a few complaints).

The tone of the responses is fun, casual, and friendly across the board. It is clear that Disney has given its social media team the leeway, or even mandate, to respond in the same way you would to a friend.

Disney Baby posts a variety of content across its social media channels: blog post links, product photos (and plugs), contests, videos, and questions that moms *love* to answer—questions such as, "When did your baby get his first tooth?" and "Any tips on making the baby to big-boy bed transition?"

With a company-wide goal of being "informational rather than commercial," it is clear that Disney chooses to focus less on products and sales and more on experiences, stories, and emotions. Thomas Smith, social media director for Disney Parks, on prdaily.com, says, "Everything we say will not be remembered, but how we make you feel will last."

This Is All Great, but What Does It Mean for My Business?

Since the size of the communities just mentioned can seem unattainable for most of us, what can we learn that we can apply to our own businesses? It is clear that each of these brands is thriving on social media. Through applying the principles of transparency and authenticity, they are consistently growing their social media presence and building relationships with their fans.

Here are eight ways these mega-brands are thriving on social media—and **how you can too**.

1. They know what their communities want.

First and foremost, each of these brands appears to have a firm grasp on what its community wants. This is hugely important. In some cases, these brands have even veered away from popular best practices, yet it is working for them. For instance, while social customer service is generally believed to be one of the most important ways brands can build trust, Starbucks and Red Bull rarely respond to comments or complaints on social media.

Red Bull seems to have found its footing within its target market, fourteen- to thirty-four-year-old males. The brand's goal is to associate its product with adventure and excitement, not with warmth or responsiveness. Because of this, those in its community are more concerned with seeing and sharing "cool" content and, in doing so, perhaps feeling a little cool themselves.

My point here is not that you should be unconcerned with social customer service. In fact, for the vast majority of businesses, I would say it should be one of your top priorities. The point is to truly know the desires of your target market, and then use social media accordingly, even if it goes against mainstream "best practices."

2. Their values come through on social media.

Each of these brands has been able to express its core business values through its social media efforts. For Starbucks, its passion for coffee, for its community, and for responsible and sustainable product sourcing is at the heart of its social strategy. For American Airlines, its commitment to superior customer service is what sets it apart.

Rather than focusing their efforts on trying to be like someone else, these companies are all true to their own brand values. In a sense, it doesn't even matter exactly *what* their values are. Whether it is building community, expressing their passion, or creating a sense of adventure, these companies excel in their own ways.

3. They don't do the hard sell—or the sell at all.

You will notice that in each of the examples, there is little, if any, selling going on. These brands know that social media is primarily social, not commercial. As I am sure you have figured out, direct selling on social media is a great way to quickly lose fans and followers! This doesn't mean you shouldn't weave in your marketing message; it simply means you should not lead with it.

Take Red Bull, for example. Not only does it do no direct sales on social media, it rarely even mentions its product. It has a clear focus: associate the brand with "cool" and adventure. By making this connection between its target market and its product, the company isn't just selling products, it is establishing connections and building lifelong loyalty. What happens as a by-product of this strategy is every time the company's ideal client thinks of something "cool and adventuresome," Red Bull comes to the top of his mind. Then what does he buy? Red Bull.

4. They mobilize brand advocates.

Although this may not be readily apparent in all of the examples listed, each of these companies relies on brand advocates to help ignite the word-of-mouth marketing it is after. Disney, for example, made a conscious decision in 2011 to use brand advocates in its global online strategy. Alan Welsman, Disney's former European marketing director, at econsultancy.com, says, "We're prioritizing social media marketing, and within that we are using Disney's Best Guests, consumers of whom we have strong social profiles, to involve them more in our offering."

Coke is going a step further, offering interested employees training in how to be a brand advocate. The company knows that at least a portion of its employees have sought out work at the company because of their love for the brand, and what better way to use this passion for the product than by offering training in how to be better word-of-mouth marketers.

5. They have a social media plan in place.

With each of these brands, it is immediately apparent that there is a social media plan or strategy in place. This is evident in a number of ways:

- The tone and "voice" of responses are uniform.
- The frequency with which comments or complaints are responded to is consistent.

- The content shared is consistent. For instance, Red Bull consistently posts photos of extreme athletes, while Starbucks consistently shares content meant to inspire passion in its product.

Having a plan in place means your social media efforts will be consistent and will decrease the likelihood of your company experiencing social media meltdowns. This is a strategy that every business—no matter how big or small—should implement.

6. They take advantage of visually based content.

Each of these brands relies heavily, if not exclusively, on visually based content. Starbucks, Red Bull, and Coca-Cola, for instance, use images on almost every one of their Facebook posts, and often use them on Twitter as well. Starbucks also has garnered a large following on image-based networks, such as Pinterest and Instagram, while Red Bull has built a huge following on YouTube.

With 40 percent[2] of people responding better to visual information than plain text, failing to offer visually based content by way of videos or images can be a costly mistake.

---

2 http://www.webmarketinggroup.co.uk/why-every-seo-strategy-needs-infographics/

7. They focus on a handful of channels.

While each of these brands has a presence on all the major social networks, all have chosen to focus the majority of their efforts on two or three. Brands know they need to be where their target market is and where their community wants to interact with them. For most brands, this is going to mean Facebook and Twitter. But, as mentioned, for brands that rely heavily on image-based content, Pinterest, Instagram, and YouTube will be particularly important.

By focusing on the most valuable and effective channels, brands can avoid wasting time and money. These brands have discovered it is better to be intentional and proactive about which networks they use than to spread themselves too thin and become ineffective.

8. They do social media in-house.

By bringing social media in-house, each of these brands has managed to maintain a social media presence in line with the goals and values of its organization. This also means its team has the knowledge and experience necessary to understand its customer base, as well as the authority to respond immediately to questions or concerns. American Airlines has taken things a step further: By integrating its social media department with its customer service and reservations departments, customers receive the highest-quality care possible.

Of course, each of the brands mentioned clearly has the budget for an in-house social media team. While this may be untenable for most small businesses, it reminds us of the importance of having a clear, consistent voice on social media. If you will be contracting out your social media, it is critical that everyone involved have a crystal-clear understanding of:

- The goal(s) of your social media efforts.
- The company culture.
- The desired voice and tone of social media posts and responses.
- When to bring a concern to management.

Final Thoughts

Throughout this chapter, I have chosen to focus on big brands that are thriving on social media; however, countless small and medium-sized businesses are using social media with great success. The point is not about gaining as many likes, fans, or followers as these brands; it is about looking at what they are doing that is working, and figuring out how we can apply those strategies to our own businesses.

Using social media successfully—and by successfully, I mean authentically and profitably—means hanging in there for the long haul and using it to achieve amazing results (whatever *amazing* means for *your* business).

EXERCISE: HOW CAN YOUR BUSINESS THRIVE ON SOCIAL MEDIA?

It is easy to feel insignificant when looking at huge brands with millions of fans and followers. However, the point of this chapter is to show you that all businesses, no matter how small, can learn from how these big brands are getting it right.

Take a few minutes to work through the eight points at the end of the chapter, and think about how you can apply each principle to your own business.

To recap, the eight points are:

1. The companies know what their communities want. What does your community want?
2. Their values come through on social media. What are your company values, and do they come through on social media?
3. They don't do the hard sell. Are you pushing your products on social media?
4. They mobilize brand advocates. Who loves your products and services, and how do you get those people involved consistently in your social media?
5. They have a social media plan in place. Do you have a defined social media plan?
6. They take advantage of visually based content. Do you use pictures and video to tell the story of your company?
7. They focus on a handful of channels. What two or three channels are you committed to?

8. They do social media in-house (or, if it's contracted out, they make sure everyone is on the same page). What resources have you committed to social media, and is everybody on the same page?

Chapter 10

BEING HEARD IN A NOISY SOCIAL WORLD

"Whether you're an entrepreneur, a small business, or a Fortune 500 company, great marketing is all about telling your story in such a way that it compels people to buy what you are selling. That's a constant."

—**Gary Vaynerchuk**, Jab, Jab, Jab, Right Hook: How to Tell Your Story in a Noisy Social World

Is it the loudest voice that gets heard on social media? The business with the most aggressive and pervasive online presence? The brand that builds the biggest following?

There is a perception that to be heard above the din, the business with the loudest "roar" wins. This couldn't be further from the truth. Being heard on social media isn't about being the loudest, dominating conversations or gaining the most attention through crazy or controversial stunts.

Throughout this book, I have tried to show how authentic brands and people win on social media—not because they are the loudest or the flashiest, but because they rely on such principles as passion, transparency, and openness to establish long-term, authentic relationships and communities. Rather than using outdated "push" methods of marketing, like loudly broadcasting their message to the masses, businesses that *attract and engage with* communities using "pull" methods stand apart from the crowd.

In a time when consumers are beyond sick and tired of being marketed to and talked at, and when they are wary and skeptical of any and every kind of brand communication ("What's the catch?"), businesses that choose to allow the principles of authenticity to govern all their actions and communications *win.*

Being heard on social media doesn't have to mean competing in the frenetic and panicked race in which many marketers are participating. You don't have to "check yourself out at the door" or fight to dominate and control the conversation. While I know letting go of control can be a scary proposition, understand there is also a great deal of freedom to be found here.

When you are able to let go of a model that says it is okay—and even expected—to control your message and your audience, you start to realize you are spending less time and energy struggling to *get yourself heard*, and more time engaging and connecting with your community.

That sounds like way more fun to me!

Being Heard Is a Process, Not a Onetime Event

In his third bestselling book, *Jab, Jab, Jab, Right Hook: How to Tell Your Story in a Noisy Social World*, my friend and social media guru Gary Vaynerchuk reminds us of the importance of being "in it" for the long haul. Anyone familiar with boxing will know the jab may not always be as glamorous or as independently effective as the right hook, but it is a necessary step in the path to the knockout. Jabbing may have to happen, again and again, before . . . POW! The fight ends with one carefully placed, powerful right hook.

In the same way, businesses need to understand the importance of balancing their marketing strategy with "jabs"—consistently creating and sharing valuable content and building relationships—and the "right hook"—campaigns that drive traffic, sales, and profits. Smart marketers know you can't have one without the other, at least not over the long term.

Gary writes:

The right hook gets all the credit for the win, but it's the ring movement and the series of well-planned jabs that come before it that sets you up for success. Without the proper combination of jabs to guide your customer—I mean, your opponent—right where you want him, your right hook could be perfect and your opponent could still dodge it as easily as a piece of dandelion fluff. Precede that perfectly executed right hook with a combination of targeted, strategic jabs, however, and you will rarely miss.

The Secret to Being Heard: Be Authentic!

You saw this one coming, didn't you?

Throughout this book, we have talked about what authentic marketers do: They know their target market, express their passion, connect with communities, and so on. But to simplify things, when it comes down to it, **being authentic is an alignment of *what you do with why and how you do it.***

We talked about the definition of "authenticity" at the beginning of chapter 1. Definitions range from "undisputed credibility" to "doing what you promise." Perhaps one of the most fitting descriptions I have come across, at least as far as the purpose of this book is concerned, is from author and leadership expert Lance Secretan. He defines it as follows: "Authenticity is the alignment of head, mouth, heart and feet—thinking, saying, feeling and doing the same thing—consistently. This builds trust, and followers love leaders they can trust."

Part of being an authentic marketer is understanding that you are responsible for how you interact with your customers and clients, all the way from point A to point X, Y, or Z. Providing well-planned, useful content (points A through X) through your blog, emails, and social media helps build the trust and respect that ultimately will lead to sales (point Z). In other words, you are responsible for the "jab" all the way through to the "right hook."

Getting heard on social media will be about maintaining your authenticity over the long term by consistently providing value and building relationships with your community. While being authentic on social media requires a firm commitment, it would be a huge mistake to think of it as overly complicated or burdensome. When it comes down to it, authenticity means staying true to the principles outlined in this book, for the long haul.

To solidify these principles in our minds, let's look briefly again at how marketers, in a time when authenticity is at a premium, can be heard amidst the noise—simply by being authentic.

Authentic Marketers Reveal Their Roots . . . and Stay Firmly Planted

Just as Burberry understands the importance of holding on to its "Britishness," authentic marketers know the value of sharing and staying true to the traits and values that make their businesses unique. Telling the story of your business's beginnings forges a connection between past and present, speaks of staying true to one's own story and of being consistent in the application of one's values.

As you tell the long-term story of your brand, you establish a sense of trust ("This isn't a fly-by-night business!") and of authenticity. You connect your brand with the past, the present, and the future. Being authentic means telling your story in a way that evokes the emotions you want associated with your brand. It means being consistent and holding true to who you are and to the foundation story of your brand.

Authentic Marketers Are Passionate

Earlier we talked about how passion is a defining feature of authentic marketing; without a true passion, both for what you do and for the people you serve, it is difficult, if not impossible, to be authentic. Work becomes a chore, and the temptation to "check your true self out" at the door becomes great. It is easy to see how this kind of passionless marketing inevitably will lead to personal and professional burnout, and to a serious loss of trust by your community.

We also talked about the difference between hype and passion: While hype is sometimes confused for the real thing, it is easy to spot when you know what to look for. Feigned, over-the-top excitement and lofty promises that can never be met may be confused with passion, but ultimately will fall flat. Hype is fragile and unsustainable; passion, on the other hand, is what gives you energy and love for what you do and for your community.

While hype always eventually fizzles out, passion is sustainable in the long term. It acts as a measuring stick to maintaining authenticity in your business; when you feel a loss of the passion you once had, you know it is time to reevaluate what you are doing or the way you are doing it. Passion drives action—it gets you up in the morning, spurs you on to greater things, and gives you the energy and dedication to keep going when things get tough.

Finally, we looked at ways marketers can leverage their passion in their social media efforts. We know passion is extremely attractive, contagious even. When you allow yourself to communicate your passion with those around you—your social advocates, your business associates, your social media followers, and your employees—it goes a long way toward building and strengthening your community.

In a time when social media is rife with businesses that will do whatever it takes to make the sale, those that maintain their authenticity through having and expressing true passion will stand out. When people recognize that you are truly passionate about your products, your business, and your community, they will want to be around you. They will choose to listen to your voice above the din because they recognize that you are authentically devoted to your business and community. People will be drawn to you, simply because you care and aren't afraid to showcase that care.

Authentic Marketers Are Just Like You

I started chapter 3 with a quote from motivational speaker Zig Ziglar: "If people like you, they'll listen to you. But if they trust you, they'll do business with you." Bottom line: People do business with people and businesses they like *and* trust.

One of the key ways to build trust and to have those in your community know you understand them is by clearly defining who your target market is and what those people value and need. What are their pain points? What problems are they looking to solve? How can your business meet those needs? It is only once you have a genuine understanding of who your customers are and what they need that you can begin to build genuine relationships with them.

By focusing on what you can give to your community—rather than on what you can get—your community begins to see that your motivations are genuine and transparent. This becomes apparent in a number of ways. Rather than being a know-it-all, you offer tentative advice and ask for feedback. Rather than bombarding your fans and followers with pushy sales messages, you ask questions, provide helpful content, and reach out to continually build new relationships. Rather than just showing up when you feel like it, you prove you are trustworthy by doing it all again and again.

When you build relationships based on transparency and trust, people on social media are more likely to be drawn to you and to want to be around you. People are unlikely to want to "hang around you" if they get the sense that you don't understand them or are using them for your own selfish gain. But when you act in ways that build trust—offering valuable content in ways they can understand and relate to, and being passionate about the things they're passionate about—you build genuine, profitable relationships that will last in the long term.

Authentic Marketers Don't Control the Conversation

A great way to make sure you *don't* get heard amidst the noise is by dominating and controlling the conversations online about your brand. While brands could get away with this just a decade or so ago, with the rise in popularity of social media, consumers know they don't need to put up with it anymore.

Authentic marketers know conversations are already happening about their products and brands online, and rather than feeling threatened or insecure or, worse, hiding their heads in the proverbial sand, they listen attentively to what's being said and acknowledge that these conversations are taking place.

Some marketers are stuck in old-fashioned and ineffective "push" methods of marketing and attempt to integrate these strategies into their social media marketing. Big mistake! Authentic marketers engage with their customers and community by asking questions, responding quickly to queries and complaints, and offering helpful content. "Bully" marketers bombard their fans and followers with pushy sales pitches and marketing messages.

In a time when consumers are sick of being "talked at"—particularly on social media—businesses that can simply *participate* in conversations, rather than attempting to control them, are far more likely to be heard.

Authentic Marketers Connect with and Build Communities

In chapter 6, we looked at some examples of successful communities, both online and offline. Communities such as Comic-Con, Harley-Davidson, and the Susan G. Komen foundation appear to be very different in many ways, at least on the surface. But what they all have in common is they *bring people together based on shared interests, visions, and passions.*

Businesses that are able to authentically connect with their own communities, as well as other people's, are on the right track. But this is only part of the equation. The other most critical part is *knowing how to behave authentically in community.* It is not enough to simply be *part of* a community on social media—you need to be a valued, transparent member. Using underhanded or pushy methods, such as spamming community members, trying to control what's said (or not said), or manipulating members into buying your products, means rapidly losing trust and risking losing your place in the community.

Authentic marketers, on the other hand, know the beauty of community is found in letting go of some of the control. In being helpful, useful, and inspiring. In using their influence to *guide* the conversation, not to control it. These traits are rare on social media, so I guarantee that if you implement them, you are sure to get noticed.

Authentic Marketers Understand Virality

Although business and marketing has changed in pretty dramatic ways over the past decade, perhaps one of the biggest changes is related to *virality.* It used to be that only big brands with big budgets could succeed; through bombarding their target market with their carefully crafted marketing messages, they could hope enough people would try their products and then tell others about them.

With the emergence of social media, however, even small businesses can reach a large audience—and a lot quicker than costly traditional methods ever could. Word-of-mouth marketing is alive and well, and hyper-accelerated through social media. Authentic marketers realize the importance of letting go of control—control of crafting marketing messages, of broadcasting them, and of telling the stories that ultimately sell their products. Virality takes the control away from marketers and puts it in the hands of consumers.

Whatever you do—good or bad—can go viral. Obviously, this can work for or against you. But when you are authentic and transparent, at least you don't have to worry about your *inauthenticity* going viral! When used appropriately, virality can be a cost-effective, extremely efficient way of getting your brand heard above the noise.

Conclusion: Will the Real You Stand Up in Social Media?

Believe it or not, being authentic on social media is a whole lot easier than being inauthentic. When you are consistent in your actions, your message, and your interactions, you don't have to be censoring or second-guessing yourself constantly:

> *Am I contradicting something I said earlier?*
>
> *How can I keep my community from seeing my true intentions?*
>
> *What happens if news of my inauthenticity goes viral?*
>
> *What do I say today?*

This type of self-talk not only is very stressful, it also signifies that you may have some work to do when it comes to establishing authenticity at every level of your business.

Being authentic on social media is a choice. It is within the grasp of every business owner—whether you run a five-thousand-dollar-per-month mom-and-pop shop or a multimillion-dollar multinational corporation. *The principles of authenticity are scalable.*

Authenticity is a choice. Allowing the *real you to stand up in social media* is a choice. In a time when authenticity is a rare commodity, it is really the *only* choice.

EXERCISE: WILL THE REAL YOU STAND UP IN SOCIAL MEDIA?

Throughout this book, I have tried to give you practical, actionable exercises to help you apply the principles of authenticity to your own business. But the fact is, completing a single simple exercise at one point will simply never be enough to set your business on the path to authenticity. Authenticity takes time, and it takes a *conscious choice.* It is a decision you must make again and again, day after day, year after year.

This exercise is one I hope you can take with you as you attempt to apply the principles of authenticity to be "heard" on social media. None of us will ever truly "be there" when it comes to authenticity—the best we can do is just keep trying our best.

1. Which principles of authenticity do you suspect will always be most difficult for you? Expressing your passion? Behaving as a valued member in

community? Letting go of the need to control the conversation? Using two ears and one mouth?

2. In what areas of your business do you see evidence of this struggle?
3. What steps or safeguards can you build into your business to help you hold true to these principles of authenticity in the long term? Greater accountability? A change in your social media procedures? A detailed action plan for avoiding missteps?

As you go about the day-to-day tasks of your business, allow the principles in this book to evidence themselves. Stay true to who you are, and vow to make integrity, transparency, and openness core values of your business. As you do, don't be surprised when you see real, rewarding results.

CPSIA information can be obtained at www.ICGtesting.com
Printed in the USA
BVOW07s1020080115

382459BV00003B/9/P